The
MINDFULNESS
Workbook

Martha Langley

For Jean and Marion.

The MINDFULNESS Workbook

Martha Langley

Contents

How to use this book

This workbook from Teach Yourself ® includes a number of special features, which have been developed to help you understand the subject more quickly and reach your goal successfully. Throughout the book, you will find these indicated by the following icons.

 Key Ideas: to make sure you grasp the most important points.

 Exercise: designed to help you to work out where you are, where you want to be and how to achieve your goals. Exercises include:

 Writing exercises - fill in your answers in the space provided.

 Quotes: Inspiring and motivating you

At the end of each chapter you will find:

  What have I learned?: helping you summarize for yourself what you can take away from each chapter.

 Where to next?: introducing you to the next step.

At the end of the book you will find:

  Task sheet: helps you highlight what you hope to achieve and ways you can go about achieving them.

 Quick help: provides you with quick solutions and useful advice that you can use in an emergency.

Introduction

→ Background

Mindfulness is a very old concept. It is a key part of Buddhism, but also appears in Hindu writings. Perhaps that sounds exotic, and even a little alien, but don't let that put you off. The concepts underlying mindfulness have been moving into Western culture for a long time. In the 1960s, The Beatles travelled to India to learn about meditation from the Maharishi, and while they were the most high profile, they were by no means the first to take an interest in Mindfulness. In the 1970s, Jon Kabat-Zinn established the Mindfulness Based Stress Reduction programme and since then other programmes, such as Mindfulness Based Cognitive Therapy, have been developed.

It's become apparent that the mindful approach to stress, anxiety and mental health problems is effective for many people. In fact in the UK, NICE (the National Institute for Health and Clinical Excellence) recommends 'mindfulness-based cognitive therapy for people who are currently well but have experienced three or more previous episodes of depression'. Mindfulness is well established in the clinical setting, where it is usually taught in groups.

Now it is gradually moving out of the clinical setting and away from its Buddhist roots into the wider community. Many people find mindful attitudes coupled with meditation help them to improve their quality of life. However, it can be easy to feel daunted, as if there is a barrier making mindfulness inaccessible. It manages to be both strange and exotic, because of its Eastern roots, and also too medical, because of the clinical approach in the West.

→ The Workbook

▶ This Workbook aims to demystify mindfulness, to take out all the jargon and make the concepts and practices accessible and easy to understand. You'll find that much of what you need to know is already part of your mindset, just under a different name. For instance, most of us understand the concept of doing something 'on autopilot'. Mindfulness suggests that you do the opposite, and calls this 'living in the moment'. Or consider these commonly used phrases:

▶ Wake up and smell the roses.

▶ Quality time.

- Count to ten.
- *Carpe diem* – seize the day!
- Don't cross your bridges till you come to them.

Or even the first lines of this well-known prayer:

> *God, give me grace to accept with serenity*
> *the things that cannot be changed,*
> *Courage to change the things*
> *which should be changed,*
> *and the Wisdom to distinguish*
> *the one from the other.*

All of these concepts are found in mindfulness, with different names but the same underlying ideas. However, mindfulness brings them together in ways that may be new to you, and it is the combinations that create the unique mindful take on life.

So if you approach the Workbook with an open mind, expecting to find simple concepts that are easy to understand, then you'll find it relatively easy to make the transition into understanding how the ideas combine to create a mindful attitude.

→ Living mindfully

While it turns out that the underlying concepts of mindfulness are familiar, and the way they are combined is accessible, there is one aspect of mindful living that can take some getting used to. There are no goals. That's right, no goals. No exams, no tick boxes, no grades or levels or stars. No winning and no losing. Almost everything we do has one or more of those aspects. If you decide to learn a musical instrument there are exams and grades. If you take up a sport there are matches or races. Even the Women's Institute will have a small competition among the members at each meeting.

Of course you can choose to play the guitar just for pleasure, or stay in the bottom team of your football club where there's little pressure to win, but the activity still brings with it the implication of your achievement being measured. With mindfulness there is none of this, there is only practice. If you meditate daily, you will find that some days you come out of the session exhilarated and walking on air, while on other days not much happens, or you even feel dissatisfied. And yet all sessions are equally valuable, and there is no comparing one with another, or monitoring your progress.

So as well as keeping an open mind, it's a good idea to let go of all striving and measuring of yourself. There are no right and wrong answers to the exercises in the Workbook, no measuring your achievement, no feeling badly if you find a chapter difficult or boring. There is just you, quietly moving towards an understanding of mindfulness, and a greater insight into yourself.

→ Using the Workbook

The Workbook is designed to be worked through from beginning to end, in the order that it is laid out. If you only read those chapters that catch your interest you'll probably find much that puzzles you, as the explanations in the early chapters are key to understanding the later chapters. The Workbook is also designed with the exercises as an integral part of the learning process. This is partly because experiencing something means much more than simply reading about it, but also because mindfulness comes to life and starts to really make sense when you practise it.

The first three chapters of the Workbook outline the core concepts of mindfulness. The exercises are designed to ease you gently in, working in small steps with plenty of explanation. At the same time you will be looking at yourself, your circumstances and your attitude to life. This will give you the level of insight you need to be able to integrate mindfulness into your own individual way of living, and also help you understand in what ways mindfulness is relevant and helpful.

There is a lot to take on board so take it step by step without rushing. If anything is unclear, reread the chapter and repeat the exercises. If an exercise seems too demanding, set your sights a little lower and repeat it several times, making small changes with each repetition. If you're still unsure after a second reading, move on and allow your mind to process what you've read – you can always return to the early chapters later, after you've experienced a little of mindfulness practice.

The next two chapters cover the more practical aspects of mindfulness, and while equally important will probably be less challenging, giving you time to grow more comfortable with what you've learnt so far.

The Workbook then moves on to explaining the various mindful practices, giving you plenty of opportunities to try them out. Once again, the small steps and detailed exercises will help you make a gradual transition into mindfulness. However as you progress the exercises gradually become less detailed, allowing you to increasingly take charge and put what you've learnt into practice.

The final two chapters look at specific ways that mindfulness can be helpful when dealing with two important aspects of all our lives today: stress and relationships. Here you will find the exercises leave even more room for you to have input.

By the time you reach the end of the Workbook you will have a good basic knowledge of mindfulness and an insight into how to assimilate it into your own life. The core practice of daily meditation leads you into feeling calmer and more centred, less stressed and more relaxed about difficulties. You'll also be able to examine aspects of your life where you feel a mindful approach would be beneficial and you'll know how to apply mindful thinking to anything from weight loss to bereavement.

There is of course much more to discover about mindfulness that the Workbook doesn't attempt to cover, but there are many other resources available. There may for instance be meditation sessions in your local community – look online or ask in your local library. There are also mindfulness retreats in various parts of the country, running for a weekend or longer.

→ Finally

It's been said that mindfulness opens up a gap between an event or emotion and your response to it. Instead of knee-jerk reactions, or quick-fix decisions, you'll find that you have time and a feeling of mental space in which you can make better decisions and wiser choices. The effects are cumulative, and once you've started, you won't want to stop.

Core concept: 'living in the moment'

In this chapter you will learn:
▶ about living on autopilot
▶ about living in the moment
▶ about the difference between Being and Doing.

→ Being and Doing and autopilot

The first key concept for mindful living is about being 'in the moment'. This means being fully engaged with what you are doing right now, whether it is pleasant or painful, important or trivial. When you are in the moment you give your full attention to what you are doing. It's astonishing how rarely most of us manage this.

 Exercise 1

THE THINGS THAT YOU DO

Think back over the last few days and create a list of some of the things you have done, taken from as broad a range as possible, covering your work, home life and social life. Include chores, challenges and interactions with other people. Use the examples in Column A to get you started, crossing out any that don't apply and adding your own items at the bottom. Leave Column B empty while you compile your list.

COLUMN A	COLUMN B
Travelling to and from work	_____
Answering the phone	_____
At your work station	_____
Lunch break	_____
Checking personal texts and emails	_____
Attending a meeting	_____
Going to the gym	_____
Going for a run	_____
Cooking dinner	_____
Phoning family members	_____
Shopping	_____
Putting children to bed	_____
Watching TV	_____
Spending time with partner	_____
Going out with friends	_____
DIY	_____
Medical appointment	_____
Surfing the web	_____
Housework	_____
_____	_____
_____	_____
_____	_____
_____	_____
_____	_____
_____	_____
_____	_____
_____	_____

Now work down your list and, in Column B, estimate how fully engaged you were with each activity, on a scale of 1–10. For instance, if you travel to work by train and spend the whole journey busy on your laptop, then that would have a very low score, but if you went out with friends and gave your whole attention to enjoying their company then give that a high score. Be honest about this – for instance if you spent time with your partner, did you give them your full attention, or were you thinking about what you needed to do next, and what was left undone at work? Did you have one eye on the TV while you listened to them? And when you read that favourite bedtime story for the umpteenth time, were you thinking about the chores still waiting to be done before you could relax for the evening?

It can be sobering to find that we are very rarely fully engaged with what is happening at the moment. The exceptions are usually when we are doing something that we love, such as a sport or a hobby, or when an emergency strikes – if your child falls and screams with pain you instantly forget everything else.

And yet if you are not engaging at other times, then you are disconnected from large chunks of your life. You are failing to experience times that you will never have again. You are living on autopilot.

The busier you are the more likely you are to be living on autopilot. You rush through your day, doing what has to be done, probably multi-tasking, and however fast you go you never seem to catch up with yourself.

Sometimes of course autopilot is useful. When you first learn a new skill, such as driving or playing the guitar, you need to be fully engaged with it just to master the basics, but later on you can switch to autopilot and focus your attention on being a better driver or musician. This is known as unconscious competence and it's the final stage of learning, when you have fully mastered a skill and can use it effortlessly. But even when you are using your unconscious competence, you can still be fully engaged with the experience.

Exercise 2

ENGAGE WITH NOW

As a first step, practise engaging with the moment right now. You are going to close the book and focus on the moment – the place you're in and the way you're feeling physically and mentally. Take your time over this and allow yourself to explore everything – how it feels to be sitting, (or lying), the air (or lack of it) on your face, the light level, the weather, any noise, any physical discomfort and so on.

Close the book and do it now.

How did that feel? Use the space below to record your reactions.

_____

_____

_____

_____

_____

_____

You may have really enjoyed the experience of simply engaging with now for a short time, but equally you may have felt jumpy and anxious about wasting time. Or maybe you found it hard to stay awake as soon as you stopped being busy.

In fact you've just briefly experienced two things – living in the moment and Being mode. Most of the time we are in Doing mode, and often on autopilot as well. Doing mode is exactly what it sounds like, the process of getting on with things.

Doing mode:

▶ is task oriented

▶ is focussed on problem solving

▶ measures achievement

- looks for successful outcomes
- is goal driven
- is critical of failure.

Doing mode is what drives humanity forwards but it's easy to forget that Being mode is important too. Not only does it give your brain a chance to take a rest from doing, it also provides the mental place where we can think about life, make decisions and work on relationships.

It is no coincidence that so many babies are born nine months after Christmas, or that so many couples file for divorce when they return from their annual holiday. A break in routine, especially a holiday, creates a small space for Being mode and the time to think about and make big life-changing decisions. But Being once or twice a year isn't enough – we need to learn to just be every day, and that is where mindfulness comes in.

There will be more opportunities to increase your understanding of being as you work through this book, but for now let's return to Doing mode and autopilot.

 *Exercise 3*

ASSESS YOUR AUTOPILOT

Revisit Exercise 1 and decide if any of your activities benefit from unconscious competence. Put a cross against anything that falls into this category. Driving is an obvious one, and if you have a highly skilled job you probably need an element of unconscious competence.

Now look at those items on the list where you can see from the low score and the absence of a cross that you were on autopilot for no good reason. Choose one of those tasks that you will do soon, today if possible, and decide to switch off the autopilot and engage fully with it. For this exercise choose something completely mundane and safe - washing up, filing, cleaning the car – and something that you will do on your own.

Coming out of autopilot: hints and tips

▶ Allow a little more time for the activity as you may be a little
slower – however you will probably also be more effective.

▶ Allow yourself to experience and appreciate every aspect of your task,
using all five senses.

▶ Do not choose an activity where there is any element of risk.

▶ If you find yourself thinking about other things, gently bring your
attention back to the task in hand.

 *Exercise 4*

SWITCHING OFF THE AUTOPILOT (1)

Undertake your task and record how it went below. Use a scale of
one to ten to measure your answers to questions 1–3.

How difficult was it to focus on just one task?

_____

How much more enjoyable than usual was the task?

_____

How much more effective were you?

_____

Did your mind wander? If it did, what were you thinking about?

_____

_____

Did you notice anything new about the task?

What did you learn from the exercise?

....

Now you've had a brief experience of coming out of autopilot when you're in Doing mode. You were still task-oriented and focussed on achieving your goals, but far more engaged with the specific job in hand. You are likely to find that you performed the task to a higher standard but the real benefit arose from being mindfully engaged with that part of your life – you really lived it, instead of just getting through it.

For the next exercise you are going to choose another item from your list that you will be able to do soon, but this time make it one that involves interacting with someone.

Coming out of autopilot: further hints and tips

▶ Allow extra time for the interaction as you may find you get talking.

▶ Choose an interaction with someone with whom you already have a positive relationship.

▶ Don't overwhelm the other person with your new focus, keep it subtle.

▶ Keep your attention kindly – this isn't a time to nag or criticize.

▶ Give your full attention and focus to the other person, without telling them why.

Exercise 5

SWITCHING OFF THE AUTOPILOT (2)

Revisit your list in Exercise 1. Choose your interaction and carry it out. Record how it went below, using a scale of one to ten to measure your answers to questions 1-3.

How difficult was it to focus on the other person?

_____

How much more enjoyable than usual was the interaction?

_____

How much more effective were you?

_____

Did your mind wander? If it did, what were you thinking about?

_____

_____

Did you notice anything new about the relationship?

_____

_____

What did you learn from the exercise?

_____

_____

_____

The experience of coming out of autopilot to connect with another person can be quite challenging, especially as they don't know what you're up to. They may be taken aback by your apparently sudden interest in them, but it's more likely that they simply lapped it up.

Even difficult relationships can be transformed if you let go of the past and simply focus on that person and what is happening between you right now. This is because part of mindfulness is to be non-judgemental – you'll learn more about this in later chapters.

→ The attraction of Doing

Letting go of Doing mode can be difficult because:

▶ Doing is fun.

▶ Exciting and challenging things happen in Doing mode – travelling, parties, job interviews, adrenaline sports. In comparison sitting quietly, on your own, meditating or just being, can seem rather tame.

▶ Doing gets you through the day. If you already feel overstretched, and each day is a rollercoaster ride of busyness, the thought of stopping for even a short time can seem too much to contemplate.

So why bother with Being mode at all?

Being mode gives you a chance for some mental rest. It's the time when you replenish your mental and emotional resources. If you don't find that immediately appealing, think of it as housekeeping for the mind. A little time spent in Being mode can produce huge benefits for the rest of your day.

You've already seen that even where Doing mode is necessary there is much to be gained by switching off the autopilot. In addition, Doing mode is not conducive to creative thinking and doesn't help you deal with unexpected problems. When people say of a problem or decision 'let me sleep on it', they are really asking for a chance to retreat into Being mode, where their mind can relax and open itself to lateral thinking.

Exercise 6

FIND A SMALL PROBLEM

Think of a problem or question you have to resolve today. Choose something small and simple, nothing life changing. For instance, 'Shall I stop off for some milk on the way home or just do without today?' or, 'Do I want to accept that dinner invitation?' or, 'Beige or taupe for the bedroom?'

Write it down here:

_____

_____

_____

_____

_____

When you are in Being mode you are:

▶ fully connected with the present moment

▶ accepting of things as they are

▶ open to all emotions

▶ tranquil, still and grounded.

Obviously this doesn't happen all at once – Being mode takes practice, and the more out of touch you have become with Being, the more practice it will take to return there. However we aren't talking years or even months – as with all skills, it's largely a question of repetition.

Exercise 7

BEING – AGAIN

In a moment you are going to repeat Exercise 2, where you put the book down and allow yourself to just be for a moment. This time, try to focus on your breathing. Don't try to change it, although it may well change of its own accord as you sit quietly observing it. Allow your mind to empty out. Imagine your thoughts are like balloons, floating in the sky. If a thought appears, you can allow it to float through your mind without trying to grab hold of it.

Now close the book and repeat the just Being exercise for a few minutes. Write down here how it went.

_____

_____

_____

_____

_____

_____

What about the little problem or question you identified in Exercise 6? If you think about it now, you may find the answer has appeared as if by magic. Don't worry if that hasn't happened. Being mode is not primarily a problem-solving technique, it's far more important than that, but sometimes it functions in that way.

→ Doing and Being and emotions

Doing mode is not helpful when you are dealing with emotional matters. In truth, it is distinctly unhelpful, because by keeping yourself busy you are keeping your emotions at a distance. When you are in Doing mode you tend to be goal oriented, looking for solutions. If you are also locked into autopilot, you'll tend to react automatically without stopping to consider, which is often bad news for relationships.

When it comes to emotional matters there are two problems associated with Doing mode:

1 In Doing mode you are too busy and rushed to truly feel your emotions, especially painful ones.

2 Quick-fix solutions are not always the most beneficial in the long term.

For instance, a person who is vaguely aware of being unhappy may well have a few glasses of wine to make the feeling go away. Doing mode is satisfied with this solution, but of course it solves nothing. It may even be the beginning of a drink problem. There are other unhelpful coping techniques such as comfort eating, looking for someone to blame or repressing emotions, but they all have the basic aim of stopping the painful emotion as quickly as possible – Doing mode looks for easy solutions.

And yet all emotions are transitory, even the painful ones, and if you just wait a while the emotion will fade, and the pain will decrease. Even a short delay – such as counting to ten if you're getting angry – can be long enough for the emotion to subside.

 *Exercise 8*

 BEING WITH YOUR EMOTIONS

Think back to the last time you experienced a mildly negative emotion – something irritating or frustrating for instance. At this stage don't choose a life-changing moment – go for 'I'm irritated that we ran out of milk' rather than 'I can't stand this job a moment longer'. Write it down here:

_____

_____

_____

_____

In a moment you are going to put the book down and spend a little time recalling that emotion. Let yourself feel it as fully as possible, but don't try to do anything about it. Try not to brood about what happened to cause the emotion. Once you have recalled the feeling, go into Being mode and sit quietly, letting yourself feel it.

Now, put the book down and do the exercise.

Use this space to record your experience

_____

_____

_____

_____

_____

→ Dealing with difficulties

For some people the switch to Being mode brings instant relief and they are immediately comfortable there. For most of us however it can seem a little strange. Here are some of the more common problems that you might encounter.

TENSION

If you are very wound up you might find it difficult to relax into just Being. You may even be a little anxious about letting go. Don't rush at it, take your time and gradually you'll learn to accept the calm that comes with Being.

FEELS TOO SLOW

The change of pace can be disconcerting. Try to stick with it for a few minutes at least, to give yourself a chance to adapt.

FEAR OF CHANGE

We all struggle sometimes with new concepts. Take your time and work in small steps – gradually you'll become more comfortable.

TOO SOLITARY

We are a sociable species, and technology means that now we are never really alone. Tell yourself that a little solitude will refresh and replenish.

UNREALISTIC EXPECTATIONS

Mindfulness is not a quick fix, and although it may be a slow fix even that isn't guaranteed. Try to let go of any expectations and approach it with a feeling of gentle curiosity.

DIFFICULT EMOTIONS RISING UP

If you've been repressing and avoiding emotions for a long time they may begin to come to the surface once you switch off the autopilot and spend some time just Being. Sooner or later those emotions will need to be dealt with, and mindfulness is a gentle and nurturing way to do this. But you could also consider looking for some extra support by finding someone to talk to, either informally (a friend or family member) or formally (a counsellor).

Developing your skills

▶ Revisit the list from Exercise 1 and add other tasks and interactions that you do on a regular basis.

▶ Each day select one task and one interaction from your list and choose to engage with them fully, coming out of autopilot.

What have I learnt?

→ What have you learnt about your how much of your life you spend on autopilot?

_____

_____

_____

_____

_____

→ What have you discovered about living in the moment?

_____

_____

_____

_____

_____

→ What have you learnt about Doing mode?

_____

_____

_____

_____

_____

→ What have you learnt about Being with your emotions?

_____

_____

_____

_____

_____

Where to next?

You've started on the journey towards understanding mindfulness and the mindful approach to life. If you learn to live fully in the moment, even during the most mundane or difficult times, you will truly live your life rather than drifting through it like a passenger. If, in addition, you start to let go of Doing and spend time just Being you'll become much more closely connected with yourself and much more appreciative of the world around you.

When you fully engage with life you'll find that feelings of happiness and contentment are more intense and satisfying, but you may worry that painful emotions will also become intense, perhaps unbearably so. In the next chapter you will learn about acknowledgement and acceptance, mindful qualities that help take the sting out of emotional pain.

Core concept: 'acknowledgement and acceptance'

In this chapter you will learn:
- ▶ about the value of acknowledgment
- ▶ about the power of acceptance
- ▶ that change is always possible.

Living in the moment has many positive aspects, but it may not be so easy to be in the moment when life gets difficult. The second mindfulness essential is acceptance, which means seeing situations in a clear way, without allowing your natural and instinctive desire to avoid pain to create foggy thinking. Acceptance allows you to be realistic, to do your best and not to waste energy on judging and criticizing yourself.

If you think about it, before you can accept something you have to understand that it exists. Acknowledgement is the first step towards acceptance.

Mindfulness means acknowledging and accepting whatever is happening in each moment, whether it is good or bad. It also means accepting yourself, as you are with all your imperfections, and accepting other people, as they are with all their imperfections.

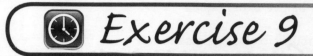

LOOKING AT DIFFICULT TIMES

Make a list of any difficult experiences you've had over the last few days. Include minor irritations as well as major annoyances, and look at the whole breadth of your life, from difficulties with technology to difficulties with other people. In the second part of the list, put any positive experiences. Again include small things and big things, across your whole life. A few examples are given to start you off. Cross out any of these that don't apply to you and then add your own. Don't write anything in column B for now.

COLUMN A   COLUMN B

Negative experiences

You overslept and were late for work.   _____

Your children were naughty in public.   _____

Toothache.   _____

You were criticized at work.   _____

Someone pushed in front of you in a queue.   _____

You broke a favourite ornament.   _____

You lost your mobile phone.   _____

Your Internet connection went down.   _____

_____   _____

_____   _____

_____   _____

_____   _____

_____   _____

Positive experiences

You were given a present. _____

You were praised at work. _____

You finished a project. _____

You did well in a test or exam. _____

Your children were praised by a teacher. _____

You found a way to solve a problem with your
home computer. _____

_____ _____

_____ _____

_____ _____

_____ _____

_____ _____

_____ _____

· ·

Before you read on, revisit your list. Is there anything you missed?
Anything that was too worrying, or too embarrassing, or too difficult to
write down? It's important to add these things. No one else needs to see
it and in the exercises for the rest of the chapter you won't be asked to
address these issues that feel so big to you. You might even need to add
something to the positives list – think about it again, just in case you
missed something.

→ Denial

So why do these extras need to be in the list at all? Simply for the purpose of acknowledgement. The bigger and more difficult an emotion or an experience is, the harder it can be to acknowledge it. We often say that someone is 'in denial', and this is something that is easy to see in other people, and easy to see how it blocks them and stops them moving forward.

For example, imagine a couple in a marriage guidance session. One of them says, 'you never listen to me'. The other one says, 'I do listen'. Stalemate. Both are convinced they are telling the truth, but clearly one of them has to be wrong, and may be in denial. Of course the denial can be on both sides. Maybe 'you never listen to me' really means 'I want my own way and I don't like it that you listen but then you disagree with me'; but equally 'I do listen' could mean 'I pretend to listen but really my mind is elsewhere'. The point is that there can be no progress until the denial stops.

The same is true in your relationship with yourself and in particular with regard to your emotions. If you try not to feel any emotion that makes you uncomfortable, then you are in denial about it and you won't be able to process it in a healthy way. What's more, the emotion will still be held inside you, simmering away and potentially causing all sorts of problems. Repressing emotions takes energy and can be a source of both anxiety and depression. If you are scared of feeling your emotions, then mindful practice can create a safe way to learn to do this.

One of the reasons why some emotions are difficult to deal with is that we judge ourselves harshly. Instead of 'I was angry', we think 'I was angry and I really shouldn't have shouted like that'.

 *Exercise 10*

LOOKING AT YOUR REACTIONS

Go back to the list from Exercise 9 and work your way through it thinking about how you reacted in each case – use Column B to describe how you felt and what you did. For instance, when you were criticized, did you get defensive or angry or upset? When you were praised, did you feel embarrassed? Don't write down anything judgemental, simply record your response. Here are some examples to get you started:

COLUMN A	COLUMN B
Negative experiences	
You overslept and were late for work.	pretended my alarm broke
Your children were naughty in a public place.	shouted at them
Positive experiences	
You were given a present.	delighted
You were praised at work.	embarrassed

Your next task is to filter out anything that is too big for you to deal with now. You can choose to return to these later, when you have progressed further into mindfulness, but don't tackle them now while you're still learning.

Exercise 11

FILTERING OUT

Look down your completed list from Exercises 9 and 10 and decide what to filter out. In Column A, you will probably want to take out anything that you added as an afterthought, because you had avoided it in the first run-through of the exercise, suggesting it is too uncomfortable to deal with right now. In Column B, look for anything where your reaction was big and unmanageable, and also look for the opposite – if you wrote 'numb' or 'shocked' as your reaction then consider filtering that item out also. If you've found it difficult to even think about these issues, just take a moment to deal with that. Say goodbye to them for now.

Once you have acknowledged something, the process of acceptance can begin. Difficult emotions and experiences often consist of two elements. There is the experience or emotion itself, and then there is your reaction to it. As well as being judgemental you may find yourself feeling guilty, sad, angry with yourself and so on. This all adds to the mental pain.

It can often be the same with physical pain. If you have toothache, you may spend a lot of energy looking for ways to make it stop, all the while clenching your jaw and resisting the pain, while at the same time frantically trying to get a dental appointment and worrying about whether the treatment will hurt. On top of the core experience of toothache you have added more pain – aching jaw muscles, panicky phonecalls, worry about the treatment.

Buddhists call this the 'second arrow of suffering' – nothing can take away the first arrow of toothache, but you can change what happens with the second arrow. In other words, once you accept the toothache and stop resisting it you will no longer have to feel the extra physical and mental pain.

The same is true of emotional pain. When you stop beating yourself up, yearning for things to be different or giving way to anger, you no longer have to feel that extra pain. Acceptance doesn't make the core pain go away, but it does make it easier to cope with.

→ Visualization

Some of the exercises in this Workbook require you to visualize an event, either recalling something that's happened in the past or imagining an event that might happen in the future. It's the same technique in both cases, although clearly with a past event memory will help you out. This will help you to be accurate, but sometimes an imaginary scenario set in the future is more powerful because your mind is freer.

The key to effective visualization is to take your time and consider every aspect in detail. These suggestions apply to all the visualizations in the book, so take the time to understand and absorb them.

Tips for visualization

▶ Close your eyes if possible – if you're reading this book in a public place, repeat the visualizations later, in private.

▶ Take a few moments to relax before you start. Let your breathing settle into a calm rhythm.

▶ Try to be inside the experience, rather than watching yourself from the outside.

▶ Create a mental picture of the environment. Where are you? Indoors or out? Are there carpets, hard flooring, desks, easy chairs? Or trees, grass, buildings, traffic? Is it heated or cold, cosy or draughty? If outside, what is the weather like? Hot or cold, wet or dry, windy or calm? Is it noisy or quiet?

▶ Sight: what can you see? Build a picture in your mind of the colours and shapes of everything around you.

▶ Smell/taste. What can you smell? Cooking, traffic fumes, freshly cut grass? Can you taste anything?

▶ Touch. Create the sensations of everything you can feel physically – your clothes, the air on your face, the texture of a seat, your hand against a surface.

▶ Create the emotions associated with the visualization. Let yourself feel them. Remember, while you are learning you won't choose to work on anything that is likely to be too difficult for you.

▶ Try not to slip into brooding – your task is to create an experience in your mind without judgement.

▶ At the end of the visualization take yourself out of it by thinking of a simple pleasure – something to eat, a favourite TV programme, a piece of music – and then return to the present moment.

▶ When the exercise asks you to repeat a visualization, don't rush it; take just as long to create it as you did the first time. You'll probably find you can add even more detail.

FIRST VISUALIZATION

It's time to choose an item from your list to work on. Run your eye down it and select something that bothered you at the time but that is no longer a big issue – one of life's minor irritations. In a moment you are going to put the book down and recreate the experience in your mind. There are three stages to this exercise:

▶ Take the time to bring the experience fully to mind, using the tips discussed to guide you. Allow yourself to feel any discomfort you felt at the time.

▶ When you've fully recreated the experience, allow yourself to let go of it and gently come out of the visualization.

When you have finished use the space below to record what happened. Pay particular attention to anything painful – give as much detail as possible. For example, don't write about an argument, 'I didn't like it', instead write, 'When he first shouted at me I was shocked, a bit numb, but then I felt my own anger unleashing. As the argument developed I felt more distressed, and after he stormed off I was shaky and upset'.

_____

_____

_____

_____

_____

_____

_____

_____

Once you have fully explored your reactions you can decide which elements were part of the second arrow of suffering. In the example given, it could be said to start at the point where 'I felt my own anger unleashing'. Perhaps simply accepting that the other person was shouting, and allowing them to run out of steam, would have prevented the pain and distress of a full-blown argument.

This example involves another person, but you may have chosen an experience that only concerned yourself. You can still analyse it to work out where the core experience ended and the second arrow of suffering took over. For instance, 'When I saw the traffic ahead of me grinding to a halt, my heart sank, and by the time we'd been queuing for five minutes I was boiling with frustration as I knew I was going to be late, the customer would be angry, and I might lose the account. I began to worry about my job, I got more and more upset.' The core experience here is the lateness caused by the traffic queue, and virtually everything that follows it is a second arrow.

 *Exercise 13*

 ANALYSE YOUR EXPERIENCE

Whatever type of experience you chose, think about how things might have turned out if your initial reaction had been acceptance rather than the knee-jerk automatic reaction that added an extra level of pain. Write down your answer here.

_____

_____

_____

_____

_____

➜ Resignation

You may find yourself resisting the idea of acceptance, on the grounds that your reaction was necessary. In the first example two people are arguing, and usually when we argue we feel justified and that we have to defend our position. You may feel that your own reaction to your experience was justified, despite the pain it caused you.

It's important to understand that acceptance is not the same as resignation or giving up. In the case of an argument, it's not a question of letting the other person win, or walk all over you, which you may feel would be the result of acceptance.

In fact, you can still manage the situation, but you choose to do it in a way that minimizes pain. As a bonus, it turns out that this is almost always a more effective approach. Assertiveness training teaches us to stay calm and focussed in difficult situations, and by accepting the initial event you are more likely to manage this.

Acceptance also creates a space in which you can assess your options. You can ask yourself questions like, 'Does it really matter if the other person wins this particular argument?' If the answer is, 'Yes, this is an important issue' then you can still look for ways to deal with it. And if the answer, as it often does, turns out to be, 'No, I'm just automatically defending my position when it really doesn't matter either way', then you can disengage before the argument even gets started.

In some situations of course there is no choice to be made. In the traffic jam example there is usually very little anyone can do (abandoning the car and walking is not usually an option). Sometimes it is possible to turn off the road and find a different route, sometimes if stationary you can at least phone ahead to say you're running late, but on the whole there is not much you can do about traffic. Of course a responsible person wants to earn enough money to finance their life, but frustration, worry about the job and anger won't help with this – they may even hinder if the person arrives at their appointment not only late but also flustered and upset. Perhaps calm acceptance, even a little resignation, is a good option here.

REPEATING THE VISUALIZATION

Now repeat the visualization, but this time recreate the scenario without the second arrow. Imagine yourself reacting to the core event with acceptance. Use the space below to record how this feels and what the possible outcome was.

_____

_____

_____

_____

_____

_____

_____

_____

Perhaps this time you felt less pain and came out of the visualization with an understanding of how acceptance can help. If you didn't, don't worry. Repeat the exercise from time to time and allow your mind to work on the concepts of acknowledgement, acceptance and the second arrow of suffering.

→ Change

If you look down your list you'll probably see that it is largely made up of things that you would like to change because in one way or another they were painful. Even the items in the 'Positives' section may have given you feelings of embarrassment or awkwardness. If we make the same response time and again, despite the discomfort it causes, there has to be a reason. This can be anything from a bad habit to deep-rooted childhood conditioning.

Change itself can seem daunting or scary ('better the devil you know' is a well-worn cliché expressing fear of change). However, with mindful acceptance it is possible to change your unhelpful responses gently. Acceptance helps you clear away the smokescreen of defensiveness, self-judging and denial and leaves the central difficulty clearly exposed.

Exercise 15

LOOKING AT CHANGE

Choose an item from your list that is ongoing for you – something that you would like to change. For instance, you may you always get upset when interacting with a specific person, or always get flustered in meetings. Start by visualizing the most recent example of this repeated behaviour. Recreate it in full in your mind, as it happened, without trying to change anything.

Now write down how it went, and how you felt. Also distinguish between the core event and the second arrow of suffering.

Core event:

_____

_____

_____

_____

_____

Second arrow:

_____

_____

_____

_____

_____

_____

_____

• •

Before you go any further, take some time to acknowledge and accept your own reactions and behaviours. It's easy to blame other people instead of taking responsibility so don't allow yourself defensive thoughts like, 'He always makes me angry' or, 'I'd be fine in meetings if she didn't try to score points all the time'. Even if you don't try to justify yourself in this way you may have a tendency to avoid facing up to what happens. So try to acknowledge, then accept, but without judging or beating yourself up.

Now consider how you would like your responses to change. This needs careful thought – you may need to look closely at your motives. For instance, here are two possible responses to the examples above:

> *Instead of bursting into tears when he gets angry I wish I could get angry too and fight back.*

> *Instead of getting flustered when she scores points in meetings I wish I could think of a quick-fire response that made her feel really small.*

Responding like this is unhelpful, a form of resistance rather than acceptance, so go back a step and spend some more time on acknowledging and accepting.

In the two examples, more mindful responses might be:

Instead of bursting into tears when he gets angry I would like to stay calm and accept that his anger belongs to him, not me.

Instead of getting flustered when she scores points in meetings I would like to stay calm and focus on the real purpose of the meeting.

Exercise 16

DECIDING TO CHANGE

Decide how you would like to change your response to your chosen situation, and write it out here:

_____

_____

_____

_____

_____

_____

_____

Now repeat the visualization but this time visualize yourself responding in your chosen way. Write down how it went:

_____

_____

_____

_____

_____

· ·

The next time you find yourself in the situation, you will have an alternative way of responding already thought through. You may not manage it the very first time, but the more often you try, the more you will work towards change.

→ Dealing with difficulties

To most of us in the West, acceptance can seem counter-intuitive. Our instinct is to get on and do something, and yet there can be a great sense of relief when we finally accept. And as you now know acceptance is the first step towards making changes.

DENIAL

No one likes to admit to what they perceive as shortcomings or failures, so denial is natural but not very helpful. Repeat the exercises as often as you need to – you may find it helps to return to them after a break.

FEELS TOO PASSIVE

This can be part of being stuck in 'Doing' mode, and the urge to take action can feel overwhelming. Finding a solution, or a quick fix, can be part of a knee-jerk response to discomfort – anything to make it go away. As you progress in mindfulness you'll find it easier to let go of 'Doing' and you'll start to explore other ways of dealing with discomfort.

FEELS LIKE GIVING UP

Sometimes doing nothing is the best option, but even if action is required, you'll make wiser decisions if you start by quietly acknowledging and accepting.

Developing your skills

▶ Revisit the list from Exercise 1 and add anything that you feel would benefit from acknowledgement and acceptance.

▶ Continue to work through the exercises.

▶ As you learn more about how this works for you, you can start to practise acceptance in real life, as events happen, instead of through visualization. Don't rush this.

What have I learnt?

➜ What have you learnt about your responses to difficult situations?

_____

_____

_____

_____

_____

➜ What have you learnt about your responses to positive situations?

_____

_____

_____

_____

_____

→ In what ways do you experience the second arrow of suffering?

_____

_____

_____

_____

_____

→ Explain the difference between acceptance and giving up.

_____

_____

_____

_____

_____

_____

Where to next?

Learning to accept what can't be changed is a normal part of growing up, although it can take a long time. Learning to accept what can be changed is a far more subtle and adult skill, and part of the skill is being able to trust that change will still be possible.

It helps to be able to stand back a little, to look at yourself objectively and let go of your emotions. The next vital mindful quality is detachment. It doesn't come easily to most people, but the next chapter will guide you through the learning process.

③ Core concept: 'detachment'

- -

In this chapter you will learn:
▶ about your relationship with your thoughts and emotions
▶ how to stand back from your thoughts and emotions
▶ about your sense of Self.

- -

One important problem associated with living on autopilot is a tendency to over-engage with your thoughts and emotions. While you are on autopilot you are not connected with whatever is going on in the moment, leaving your mind free to brood about the past or fantasize about the future. This can be thoughts, or emotions, or both. Even when you learn to come out of autopilot, you can still find yourself overly engaged with what is going on inside your head. Mindful detachment gives you a way of working with these habits. It creates a sense of perspective and frees up energy.

 Exercise 17

 IDENTIFYING WHERE YOU ENGAGE

Look back at the two lists you have already made (in Chapters 1 and 2) and choose items that you know you tend to become very engaged with, either emotionally or in your thoughts or both. Write them under Column A, and add any new ones that occur to you. Leave column B empty for now. There are some examples to give you the idea.

COLUMN A	COLUMN B
Attending a meeting.	_____
Medical appointment.	_____
Your children were naughty in public.	_____
You were praised at work.	_____
Driving, someone cut in front of you.	_____
Weighing yourself.	_____
Making a speech.	_____
_____	_____
_____	_____
_____	_____
_____	_____
_____	_____
_____	_____
_____	_____

· ·

If you remember, in Chapter 1 you practised letting thoughts float through your mind like balloons drifting in the sky. With some thoughts this is easy, but others insistently demand your attention. It's the same with emotions – some will die away quickly, but others will last a little longer. For the next exercise pay attention to both the nature of your response and how long it lasted.

Exercise 18

IDENTIFYING YOUR RESPONSES

Go back to the list and use Column B to describe your responses – recall how you were feeling and what you were thinking, and whether it was short-lived or tended to linger. Here are the examples to get you started:

COLUMN A	COLUMN B
Attending a meeting.	couldn't sleep the night before
Medical appointment.	worried about it all week
Your children were naughty in public.	embarrassed, ruined the day
You were praised at work.	had to tell everyone!
Driving, someone cut in front of you.	furious, seething afterwards
Weighing yourself.	dreaded it, OK afterwards
Making a speech.	chickened out in the end

You can see that in the examples that the response was either about a past event (the last four examples) or the anticipation of a future event (the first three examples).

Next you are going to choose an item from your list where your response went on for a while. It can be something that you couldn't let go of after the event, or something that you focussed on before the event, but at this stage don't choose anything that was exceptionally difficult for you, such as a bereavement.

Exercise 19

RECREATING THE EXPERIENCE

Use your visualization techniques to recreate the experience in your mind. Remember not to rush the early stages – build up a picture in your mind of the place, the time, the sights and the sounds. Then allow your mind to move away from the picture you've created, forwards or backwards in time so you can recreate either your anticipation or your response after the event. Again, take your time and recreate your feelings and thoughts.

After you've finished the visualization, make notes about your response. It might help to ask yourself the following questions:

How long did my response last?

How intense was it?

What were my thoughts?

What emotions was I feeling?

Did I keep coming back to it?

Where in my body did I feel it?

Use the space below to write down what you discovered about your response:

_____

_____

_____

_____

_____

_____

Let's take the example of someone whose children were naughty in public – running round at the supermarket perhaps, pulling things off the shelves, and maybe having a tantrum when they were corrected. She might write:

> *I was so furious I told the kids no sweets for a week. I was seething for the rest of the day, very angry. Couldn't settle to anything, and during my evening class my mind kept wandering. Couldn't sleep that night, wondering if I was a bad parent, what was going wrong.*

Two things are going on here – emotions (anger, guilt) and thoughts (brooding about being a bad parent). Neither of these are helpful, indeed the anger ruined the evening class session and the brooding lead to a lost night's sleep. It would only take a few more experiences like this to make life thoroughly miserable.

MORE VISUALIZATION

Choose three further items from your list and repeat the visualizations. For each one, write down what you learn about your responses.

1 _____

_____

_____

_____

2 _____

_____

_____

_____

3 _____

_____

_____

_____

∙∙

→ Understanding your unhelpful mental habits

Now that you've looked at four of the items on your list you can begin to build up a picture of your mental habits. Perhaps you tend to brood after an event, or perhaps you're more likely to dread it beforehand and feel only relief afterwards. Maybe your emotions sweep you up and carry you helplessly along, so that you feel quite powerless. If you can't see a pattern emerging, don't worry, just carry on working through the chapter.

THOUGHTS

If you tend to ruminate and let your thoughts run away with you, then they are likely to fall into one of the following categories.

Judgemental thoughts like:

▶ 'I'm so useless.'

▶ 'I always get it wrong.'

▶ 'It's my fault.'

Hopeless thoughts like:

▶ 'Everything's against me.'

▶ 'Everyone laughs at me behind my back.'

▶ 'I never feel up to it.'

Perfectionist thoughts like:

▶ 'I should have got it right.'

▶ 'I should be doing better than this.'

▶ 'If it's not absolutely right then I've failed completely.'

Anticipatory thoughts like:

▶ 'What if it all goes wrong.'

▶ 'What if I do something stupid.'

▶ 'Nobody will like me.'

Unrealistic expectations such as:

▶ 'I'll have the best time ever.'

▶ 'Nothing can go wrong.'

Exercise 21

LOOKING AT YOUR THOUGHTS

Examine the notes you made about your thought responses and see if there is a pattern, or a dominant mental habit, or habits. Use the space below to make notes.

_____

_____

_____

_____

_____

_____

EMOTIONS

Perhaps you are adrift on a sea of unhelpful emotions such as fear, anger, jealousy and embarrassment and it feels as if they are in control.

Simple emotions such as anger and fear are an instant response to what is happening in the moment and are designed to be short-lived, although sometimes we develop the habit of holding on to them.

More complex emotions such as jealousy and embarrassment are longer lasting (although even they will die down if left alone) and they are part of your wider mental landscape, formed by your childhood, your culture and your experience of the world.

As an example, not everyone is embarrassed by the same things, and the concept of what is embarrassing varies from culture to culture and across time. For instance, most English people would feel too embarrassed to share a lavatory with another person, and yet in medieval England communal facilities were the norm, as they still are in other parts of the world.

 Exercise 22

LOOKING AT YOUR EMOTIONS

Examine the notes you made about your emotional responses and see if there is a pattern, or a dominant emotional habit or habits. Use the space below to make notes.

_____

_____

_____

_____

_____

_____

Now that you have some insight into your own mental and emotional habits you may be able to see that it would be helpful to be less engaged with them. By taking a step back you will become more aware of just what it is you do and in what ways your responses are unhelpful, and you'll start to see that there is a possibility of change.

Exercise 23

WATCHING YOURSELF

Choose one of your visualizations that was particularly powerful and recreate it. This time, however, you are not going to be inside the experience. Instead you will be watching, as if you were in the theatre or watching TV or a movie. Be sure that you include everything your central character (that is, you) is thinking and feeling – you could add a voiceover to create this.

Afterwards make notes about the experience:

_____

_____

_____

_____

_____

_____

Of course when you watch something in this way you are not a neutral observer, in fact you're quite likely to have strong judgements about the scene unrolling in front of you. Watching yourself like this and seeing your behaviour from the outside can easily lead you into judging and criticizing yourself. Or you may become defensive and blame other people for what happened. Don't let yourself become depressed about what you saw of yourself in the exercise – mindfulness encourages you to be gentle with yourself.

It helps to achieve true detachment if you can create a little space in your mind where you can quietly watch what is going on. One way to learn how to do this is to create an observer. This person is a version of you, but calmer. Someone who doesn't judge, or get involved with what's going on, but who takes a gentle and kindly interest in you. And above all someone who most definitely doesn't share your unhelpful mental habits. If it helps you can imagine what they look like – an older wiser version of you would be good – but this isn't essential.

⏰ Exercise 24

CREATING AN OBSERVER

Now repeat the visualization from Exercise 23, but imagine you are the observer. Watch the scene as it unfolds, watch yourself reacting and responding. Don't judge, or criticize. Just be the observer.

After you've finished the visualization, ask yourself the following questions:

What did the observer see during the actual event?

What did they note of the time before the event, or after the event? (This depends of course on which type of event you chose to work on.)

Use the space below to write down what you discovered about the observer's response:

_____

_____

_____

_____

_____

_____

_____

_____

In the example of the naughty children in the supermarket, the observer might have written:

> *I saw a woman in a rush whose children were tired and seemed to be playing up. She was clearly embarrassed when people noticed this, although she had no way of knowing what those people were really thinking. She became irritated, and then angry, and the children's behaviour was even worse. Later on I observed her worrying about the event, reliving it, and being thoroughly miserable. Her worry and brooding didn't seem to produce any helpful insights.*

It's important to remember that the observer is part of you, a part, what's more, that only wants the best for you. The observer doesn't criticize, or judge, and has a strong desire for you to be happy and fulfilled. If you find it difficult to create this quality of loving kindness towards yourself, spend some time thinking about where you have come across it elsewhere. When you were growing up, perhaps there was an adult who saw only the best in you – grandparents are often like this, or aunts and uncles. Or maybe you've felt like that yourself, towards a child, or a pet. It's important to identify and engage with that feeling of unconditional positive regard for yourself. If you are very locked in to self-criticism then it may take a while to achieve this, but persevere.

Exercise 25

MORE OBSERVING

Repeat the observer exercise with three more events, and use the space below to make notes. Remember that the observer is not part of the events, doesn't judge, and wants you to be happy.

1 _____

_____

_____

_____

_____

2 _____

_____

_____

_____

_____

3 _____

_____

_____

_____

_____

→ Where are you?

If you were asked to describe yourself in ten words, what would you say? Try it now in the following exercise.

DESCRIBE YOURSELF

Describe yourself in ten words or less. It doesn't have to be a formal sentence.

_____

_____

_____

_____

_____

_____

What did you choose? Your appearance – 'tall, skinny, brown hair'? Your roles in life – 'IT consultant, father of three, chair of local allotment association'? Your personal qualities – 'hardworking, tolerant, untidy'? Or maybe a mixture of all three? And where is the real you? Would our IT consultant's children recognize their easygoing father if they could see him at work solving a system crash?

The point of this exercise is to help you work out where you think your sense of who you are – your sense of Self – is located. It's unlikely that you included anything about your thoughts and emotions in your description because you instinctively know that these are short-lived. So the mother of the naughty children from the example above would not have described herself as 'angry, and worried, I'm a bad parent' because both of those things will pass.

She might though have written 'a bit of a worrier' if she recognized that tendency in herself, but even that wouldn't take her into the core of her sense of Self. It's just a mental habit.

Despite this, many people, without really thinking it through, feel that here is a strong connection between their thoughts and/or their emotions, and their sense of Self.

In mindfulness it is suggested that this doesn't have to be the case. In other words:

▶ You are not your thoughts.
▶ You are not your emotions.

Both are part of you, but they are not the essence of who you are, merely an aspect of it. If you can think of your Self as quite separate from your thoughts and emotions, then detachment becomes easier. What's more, negative thoughts and difficult emotions start to lose their power over you.

Many emotions are uncomfortable – even excessive joy can be painful. As with any form of discomfort, our instinctive reaction is to do something to make it go away. There is a certain relief in slamming a door or bursting into tears. For some people food or alcohol help ease the pain.

 *Exercise 27*

RELIVING AN EMOTION

Choose an item from your list that had a definite emotional content, rather than one that was driven by thoughts. Spend a little time reliving that emotion (use visualization if that helps). Once you have recaptured how you were feeling, think about how you dealt with the emotional aspect of the experience and in particular what you did to make yourself feel better.

Make notes here:

_____

_____

_____

_____

_____

_____

Are you, like most of us, dealing with your emotions while you are in Doing mode? Are you also on autopilot? A knee-jerk reaction rarely produces a good response. In Doing mode you will be looking for solutions ('I need to make this pain stop') and setting goals ('I need to make it stop now'). If you switch to Being mode then you can let your emotions just Be, and let them run their natural course.

Of course the emotions will still be painful, but there is a mindfulness technique that helps soothe the pain – 'breathing into'. It's a useful technique that can be used in many ways and like all new skills it needs practice. You focus your attention on part of your body, breathe quietly and as you breathe in imagine your breath travelling to that part of your body. Repeat for several breaths.

Exercise 28

'BREATHING INTO'

Choose a part of your body, a hand or finger perhaps, and breathe into it.
....

When you are breathing into an emotion, first identify the part of your body where you are feeling the emotion and then breathe into it. Imagine your breath calming and soothing you.

Exercise 29

BREATHING INTO AN EMOTION

Repeat Exercise 27, recreating a difficult emotion. This time imagine yourself accepting the emotion, being with it, breathing into it and watching it quietly while it runs its course. Don't judge yourself or criticize.

Make notes here:

_____

_____

Core concept: 'detachment'

_____

_____

_____

_____

···

→ **Dealing with difficulties**

DETACHMENT FEELS TOO COLD

Detachment isn't about being cold or uncaring. Imagine yourself trying to comfort a crying child – does it help them if you start crying too? No, it's better if you remain calm.

IT'S TOO HARD TO LET GO OF MENTAL HABITS

Give yourself time. You may be working on something that is too big for you – look for a smaller, less distressing event to start with.

DETACHING FROM THOUGHTS AND EMOTIONS FEELS LIKE LETTING GO OF YOUR SELF

Your thoughts and emotions aren't you, and gradually you will learn to trust that this is so. Just do what you can for now.

YOU DON'T FEEL YOU DESERVE LOVING KINDNESS

If you can't convince yourself that you deserve this, just do it anyway and see what happens.

What have I learnt?

→ What have you learnt about your emotional responses?

_____

_____

_____

_____

_____

→ What have you learnt about your responses to thoughts?

_____

_____

_____

_____

_____

→ What have you learnt by observing yourself?

_____

_____

_____

_____

→ What have you learnt about your unhelpful mental habits?

_____

_____

_____

_____

Where to next?

You now have some insight into all three key mindfulness qualities: living in the moment, acceptance and detachment, and you've begun to experience simply Being. If you feel uncertain about any of these, go back and reread Chapters 1– 3, repeating the exercises and generally consolidating your understanding. However there's no need to feel you have reached a total understanding of anything that's unfamiliar to you – sometimes it helps to let your mind work on new ideas without your conscious involvement.

The next chapter looks at the logistics of preparing yourself for formal mindfulness practices. These may seem simple, and largely they are, but if you take the time to work out the details you'll find it makes a big difference.

4 Physical preparation

In this chapter you will learn:
▶ about the best environment for meditation
▶ how to choose a posture for meditation
▶ about the requirements for the three-minute breathing space and the body scan.

The various techniques that can help you towards mindfulness all bring with them a degree of commitment and also some practical requirements. The good news is that you don't have to spend money on any special equipment, but you do need to give some thought to other needs. Although these are quite simple, they can sometimes present unexpected difficulties.

 Exercise 30

CHECKLIST

Start by answering a few basic questions:

How much time are you able to give to mindfulness exercises and meditation?

_____

Do you have access to a private space?

_____

Will the people you live with respect your need for undisturbed time?

_____

Are you able to sit or kneel with your back unsupported?

_____

Can you manage with your mobile phone turned off?

_____

Do you dislike solitude?

_____

Do you dislike silence?

_____

··

→ Requirements for meditation

TIME

There is a lot of flexibility in the amount of time you give to meditation but there is a clear correlation between time and benefits – in other words, the more you put in, the more you get out. However the most important thing is to make a commitment and stick to it, and the most important commitment is to meditate every day, even if only for a short time.

First, think about your weekly routine. Many of us have a different routine for weekdays and weekends, but there are other patterns. If you're a shift worker, or you don't work, your routine will be different. If you have very young children all days may be much the same due to their demands, but if you have school age children the holidays will be very different from term-time.

 *Exercise 31*

YOUR WEEK

Make brief notes about how your week generally pans out, looking particularly at your various commitments:

Monday _____

_____

Tuesday _____

_____

Wednesday _____

_____

Thursday _____

_____

Friday _____

_____

Saturday _____

_____

Sunday _____

_____

Good times to meditate are first thing in the morning, before you start your day, and in the early evening, before you start to wind down towards bedtime. It is tempting to use meditation as part of your pre-bedtime routine but on the whole this doesn't work well. You might fall asleep inadvertently, or at the other extreme many people come out of meditation feeling highly energized and unable to sleep. If you feel you can't arrange to meditate at either of the ideal times then look for a time that does suit you.

Ideally you will need 30 to 45 minutes for meditation, which includes time to settle into it and time to emerge gently, although at first your sessions will be much shorter. If you can't find that much time then decide what you can manage and commit to that. You'll feel better if you choose, say, ten minutes and keep to that, than if you choose 30 minutes and only do ten. If it can be at the same time each day so much the better, but again, if that isn't possible, then do what you can.

Whenever you decide is your time for meditation, bear in mind that it will need to be when you can be sure of privacy and no interruptions. If you have caring responsibilities you'll need to think about who will cover for you.

Exercise 32

TIMES FOR MEDITATION

Consider each day and decide when you are going to include the time for meditation:

Monday _____

_____

Tuesday _____

_____

Wednesday _____

_____

Thursday _____

_____

Friday _____

_____

Saturday _____

_____

Sunday _____

_____

PLACE

It is likely that you'll choose to meditate at home, on your own, during your free time. In some parts of the country there are meditation sessions, usually run by Buddhist monks, where you can go for an hour or so and be taken through a guided meditation. However these are often only weekly, or even fortnightly and are no substitute for daily solitary meditation.

Give some thought to where you will do your meditation. Busy rooms such as living rooms and kitchens are unlikely to be private enough, and most people choose a bedroom or spare room – work out what would suit you and your family or housemates best. Now consider the room in more detail:

 *Exercise 33*

MEDITATION ROOM

Is the room private? ☐

Can you have sole use of it for the required time every day? ☐

Is it warm enough (you'll be sitting still, and could easily become chilled) ☐

Can you turn off all electronics such as TVs and computers, and unplug the phone? ☐

Is there space to sit or kneel – a chair, low stool or floor space with a carpet or rug on it (see below for more on this)? ☐

Can you create a subdued light level? ☐

You may find it feels a little odd to be in your home and yet not available, and the people you live with may take a while to learn that they can't have your attention during your meditation time. This applies to adults as much as children and teenagers – it's just a question of establishing a new habit for all of you.

Before each session spend a little time quietly organizing the room - repeating the same actions each time will create a little ritual that will help ease you into the right frame of mind for meditation. In some traditions a little bell is rung to signal the start of meditation – if that appeals to you then keep one in the room.

 *Exercise 34*

TRIAL RUN

Organize your chosen room as if for meditation – warm, private, all electronics switched off, phone unplugged, subdued lighting. Spend a little time there alone to be sure you are comfortable. Choose where you will meditate, if possible a place that allows you to rest your gaze on something pleasant but emotionally neutral – a vase of flowers rather than a photograph of a family member. If you can, have your back to the window.

PHYSICAL

There are many different postures that can be adopted for meditation, and opinions differ over what is best, but the prime requirement is to be able to sit or kneel with your back unsupported. Meditation is not a form of relaxation or rest, and so there is no leaning back against cushions or even the back of a hard chair.

However if you have a health problem that stops you holding yourself upright, then you can still meditate. You will find it harder to stay awake, and harder to achieve the meditative state of being alert and yet tranquil, but if you take it gently and don't rush yourself you will still get there.

⏰ *Exercise 35*

SITTING WITH UNSUPPORTED BACK

If your health permits, practise sitting with an unsupported back for a short time – you can do this while doing something such as eating, watching TV or, of course, reading this book. Remember, it won't work if you are leaning forward over a keyboard or machine.

Traditional Eastern meditation poses involve sitting on the floor in a cross-legged posture, sometimes with one foot on the opposite thigh, sometimes with both feet raised onto the thighs (half or full lotus positions). The discipline requires the meditator to maintain the posture however uncomfortable.

Western mindfulness is less stringent, and while you can sit in a lotus position if you are able to, there are other options. You can kneel, with either a small cushion or low meditation stool supporting your backside, or you can sit on a chair or stool. When sitting you need to have both feet flat on the floor, with your hips higher than your knees if possible (you can prop up the back legs of the chair or stool to help achieve this).

It's important to balance your head on your spine in a neutral position, so that there is no muscular strain. This can feel awkward at first, as most of us spend a lot of time angled forwards, and often support the head by leaning on something, for example propping your chin in the palm of one hand while using the other hand to hold the phone or book.

TRYING OUT POSTURES

Try various postures for meditation until you find one that seems likely to suit you. Try each one for several minutes before deciding what will work best for you.

• •

Whatever your chosen posture, it is generally referred to as 'sitting'.

Body language reflects our feelings, but also feelings can follow body language. The postures for meditation are all stable and balanced so that your mood will follow. For the same reason, it's important to sit with your head balanced centrally on your spine, your shoulders open and back, your legs relaxed. Keep your hands open and relaxed, no clenched fists. You can rest your hands on your knees, with the palms either up or down, or rest your arms across your thighs, with your fingertips touching.

BALANCING YOUR HEAD

Sit in your chosen posture and focus your attention on your head. Lean gently from side to side a few times, until you identify a central point where your head is balanced. Then move gently backwards and forwards and find the point of balance again. You may need to repeat this a few times. Consciously relax your neck and shoulders.

• •

Traditionally meditators do not close their eyes. Instead, they allow the lids to half close, and gaze without focus slightly downwards. In the West, however, people often seem to feel more comfortable with their eyes fully closed. There is a risk though that you will start snoozing or daydreaming, and generally your mind is more likely to wander when your eyes are closed.

It makes sense to give some thought to your bodily needs while you meditate. While 30 to 45 minutes isn't a great deal of time, it is best to have an unbroken session – no comfort breaks! Make sure that you won't be hungry, or thirsty, or need the toilet during your meditation. On the other hand, don't meditate on a full stomach.

Choose what you will wear – clothing should be loose and comfortable, especially round the waist. If possible keep a set of clothes just for your meditation time – as you change into them you will start to get into the right mood. Wear socks to keep your feet warm, but no shoes.

 *Exercise 38*

 ## PRACTICE SESSION

Spend a few minutes sitting quietly in your chosen place, in your chosen posture, with eyes half closed and your gaze unfocussed. Don't try to meditate, just explore how it feels to sit like this. Note: If you are continuing to work on the visualizations, avoid using your chosen place, time and meditation posture for these.

Afterwards use the space below to record your thoughts about the experience:

_____

_____

_____

_____

_____

_____

_____

→ Requirements for other mindful techniques

Formal meditation is the basis of all mindfulness, but you will also be learning two other techniques: body scan and the three-minute breathing space (see Chapters 7 and 8). The requirements for these are less rigorous and also less time consuming, although while you are learning to do them you might need to treat them more formally – once mastered they are both available to you in many everyday situations.

→ Body scan

TIME

Body scan can take anything from a few minutes to half an hour, it's very much up to you. Once you have learnt the technique (see Chapter 7) you will probably find yourself using it for short sessions quite regularly with occasional longer slower sessions. There is no need for a regular commitment and no preferred time of day.

PLACE

You do need a degree of privacy for a body scan; you should be able to sit or lie comfortably and you must be in a place where you feel safe. You, however, don't need a special room and you don't have to make formal arrangements to avoid interruption. Once you are familiar with the technique you'll be able to do a body scan with eyes open in, for example, a public place, but this will never be quite as effective. You won't be able to do it while driving, operating machinery or doing anything else where safety is a consideration.

PHYSICAL

Unlike meditation, a body scan is carried out in a comfortable position either lying down or sitting and leaning against a support. There is no special posture, and you will probably find body scan easier with your eyes closed. There is no special clothing, but if you are wearing anything constricting it will help to loosen it slightly, especially round the waist. Be sure that you'll be warm enough, use a blanket if necessary. If possible take your shoes off.

→ Three-minute breathing space

TIME

As the name suggests this technique takes about three minutes (see Chapter 8 for full explanation of the technique), however it can be extended a little, or reduced to as little as the space of three breaths.

PLACE

You can do a three-minute breathing space almost anywhere, although your attention will be on yourself rather than anything external such as a conversation. Turn off your mobile phone if possible. Once again you won't be able to do it while driving, operating machinery or doing anything else where safety is a consideration.

PHYSICAL

There is no special posture and no need to close your eyes. You don't have to lie or sit, although you may find it easier to do so. Make yourself as comfortable physically as possible, but don't get into a position for sleep. Sitting up, with your feet on the floor, is a good posture.

→ Dealing with difficulties

PHYSICAL DISCOMFORT

During meditation this is inevitable when you sit for a long time, especially if you are not used to it. Try to tolerate it. Breathe into the discomfort and accept it. If you really can't go on, make the decision to move, then gently move, stretch, and then return to the posture for a little longer. (Even a return of only a few minutes will start to teach your mind and body that you are serious in your commitment to meditation). You are unlikely to feel discomfort during body scans or breathing spaces.

WORRY ABOUT COMMITMENT

In a busy life it can seem impossible to find time for meditation. However, it is less daunting if you set an initial limit. You need to give mindfulness a chance and a few days or even a couple of weeks won't be long enough for you to decide whether it's for you. When meditation is taught as part of other therapies, courses often run for eight weeks, so why not commit to trying it for that long.

WORRY ABOUT PRIVACY

Many more people live alone now than ever before, but at the same time living space is getting smaller and many homes are pretty crowded. If necessary negotiate with the people you live with to have exclusive use of a room for a short while each day.

WORRY ABOUT POSTURE

Even without health issues you may find it difficult to sit with an unsupported back for any length of time. The more you do it, the better you'll be able to tolerate it – and you'll be improving your general posture as a beneficial side-effect. However don't push yourself beyond reasonable limits; allow your body time to adjust to your new habit.

DISPLACEMENT ACTIVITIES

While it's important to give due consideration to all the aspects covered in this chapter, do beware of finding excuses not to get started. Do the best you can with the room, time, clothing, posture and so on but don't let yourself wait until they are all perfect.

Developing your skills

▶ Revisit the list of questions in Exercise 30 and revise your answers in the light of what you've learnt.

▶ Repeat any exercises that you feel the need to, but focus on Exercise 38, extending the time that you sit quietly for. You can listen to music or to the radio while you get used to both the posture and the solitude, but don't make phone calls or send texts or emails.

What have I learnt?

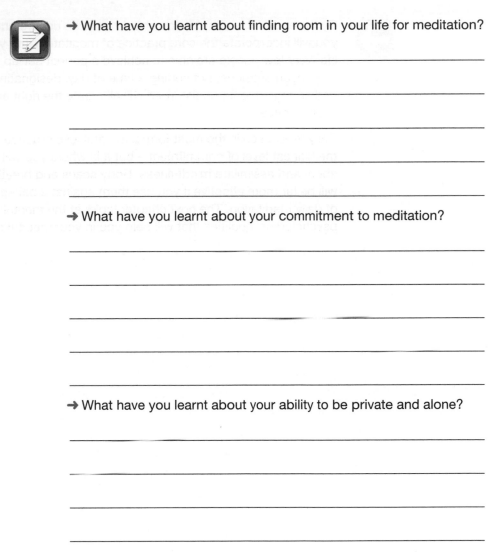

➜ What have you learnt about finding room in your life for meditation?

_____

_____

_____

_____

➜ What have you learnt about your commitment to meditation?

_____

_____

_____

_____

➜ What have you learnt about your ability to be private and alone?

_____

_____

_____

_____

Where to next?

By the end of this chapter you should have an understanding of how you will incorporate the core practice of meditation into your daily life. Very few people are able to achieve a perfect set-up for their meditation sessions, but setting a time of day, designating a place and arranging to be undisturbed will all create the right ambience for your practice.

Daily meditation is the most formal mindfulness practice, and requires the highest level of commitment – but it is where you will really learn about and assimilate mindfulness. Body scans and breathing spaces will be far more effective if you use them against a background of daily meditation. The next chapter looks at the mental and psychological qualities that will help you in your meditation practice.

5 Mental preparation

In this chapter you will learn:
▶ about the qualities needed for mindfulness
▶ how to prepare mentally for meditation
▶ to let go of judging yourself.

You can be sure that you already have all the qualities needed for mindfulness and meditation. Everyone does, and the more you practise the more you will develop the patience, acceptance, focus and concentration that are needed. It's helpful to approach mindfulness with a positive attitude. Of course you may feel some apprehension, or may not be convinced of the value of mindfulness, but that needn't stop you keeping an open and curious mind.

 Exercise 39

WHERE ARE YOU AT MENTALLY?

Are you easily bored? ☐

Do you find it hard to tolerate physical discomfort? ☐

Are you goal driven? ☐

Do you hate routine? ☐

Do you struggle to concentrate? ☐

Are you easily distracted? ☐

Do you feel you have to be always on call? ☐

Don't judge yourself based on your answers or decide that you'll be hopeless at mindfulness if you have ticked a lot of boxes. These answers simply help you understand some aspects of you as you are now. Whatever picture emerges from your answers, accept it, and accept also that there is no success or failure in mindfulness, so it follows that there is also no 'hopeless'. There is just you, starting on your journey from wherever you happen to be.

To find out exactly what your starting point is, analyse the answers you ticked.

→ Boredom and restlessness

If you are always busy multi-tasking and juggling, then it can feel very strange to stop and do nothing. Your mind keeps racing, and before you know it you've checked an email, sent a text or added something to your 'to do' list as well as, perhaps, drinking a coffee and holding a conversation. No wonder when you switch to sitting quietly on your own it is hard to slow down. At first your mind will be crowded with thoughts and it may even feel that you are wasting time.

You'll find that some days this will be more extreme than others but whatever is happening on that day accept that it is the case. If you start to feel bored and restless during a meditation session acknowledge it, and spend a little time observing, without judging. Allow yourself to feel the feelings, and accept that they are uncomfortable. Instead of getting rid of them by Doing, gently remind yourself that you made a commitment to meditate. You may find that the feelings subside, but if they don't, see how long you can tolerate them for. Tell yourself that it will be an interesting experience.

If you really must take a break, let it be a conscious decision rather than a knee-jerk response. Come out of your meditation, stand up, take a few moments to calm yourself and then return to the meditation. If you do this it will signal to your rebellious mind that you are serious in your commitment. Over time your mind will accept meditation and you will have learnt patience.

Use the space below to make notes about your attitude to boredom and restlessness, and how you plan to approach this:

_____

_____

_____

_____

_____

_____

→ # Physical discomfort

As you already know from Chapter 4, sitting in one position for any length of time can become uncomfortable – a knee or a hip may start to ache, or you may long to lean back and relax your spine. If you start with short sessions and build up gradually you will increase your ability to hold your position, but even so there may be times when the discomfort distracts you mentally from meditating.

Allow yourself to feel the physical sensations, and accept that they are uncomfortable. You may find that the feelings subside, but if they don't, just like with boredom, see how long you can tolerate them for. Tell yourself that it will be an interesting experience, and that you won't push yourself beyond reasonable limits. If you really must take a break, let it be a conscious decision rather than a knee-jerk response. Come out of your meditation, stand up, stretch or move the aching part and then return to the meditation.

Use the space below to make notes about your attitude to physical discomfort, and how you plan to approach this:

_____

_____

_____

_____

_____

_____

→ Goals

If you are goal-driven then meditation can leave you feeling that it has no point, nothing to work towards. You can't measure your achievement, and instead of striving to improve, you are encouraged to accept your performance without judging. Without goals to focus on you can feel vulnerable and disorientated.

If you need a practical justification for an activity without goals, bear in mind that goals by definition produce the concepts of success and failure, which are a huge part of our tendency to be self-judgemental. If you feel you've succeeded, then there is nothing else to do, if you feel you've failed, then you make yourself miserable. Moreover, if you go into mindfulness feeling challenged, and fearing failure, you'll only make it more difficult to embrace. Pre-judging anything can affect the outcome, so try to maintain a neutral, interested stance.

If you look at the various goals that dominate your life (better job, more money, better time management, weight loss, fitness, more material possessions and so on) you will see that behind them all is the desire to be happy. There are no guarantees with mindfulness, and no promises, but there is the possibility that you will become happier.

Use the space below to make notes about your attitude to the lack of goals, and how you plan to approach this:

_____

_____

_____

_____

_____

_____

→ Routine

Life is dominated by routines, some of which we seem to accept (cleaning teeth) and some of which can become tedious (the daily commute perhaps). Some people feel safer following a set routine, others need constant variety. In the early stages of learning about meditation there is no doubt that an element of routine is helpful. If you make meditation one of the routines that you accept then it will quickly become part of your life.

In fact, you will find that it is only your outward behaviours that are routine, because every meditation session is different. The routine works best if it is slightly ritualized, so that you always ease yourself into a session in the same way and as far as possible at the same time of day. It's quite common for actors, musicians and athletes to have routines as a way of putting themselves into the right frame of mind for the unpredictable challenges ahead, and meditation is much the same.

Having a routine also means that you build the essential element of repetition in to your practice. In recent years brain scans have shown how repetition actually helps build skills by establishing new neural pathways and connections. When you are learning a new skill, or getting to grips with a new concept, regular repetition seems to be the key.

Use the space below to make notes about your attitude to routine, and how you plan to approach this:

_____

_____

_____

_____

_____

_____

→ # Concentration

When you're meditating there is nothing specific to focus on, apart from your breathing, so concentration in the normal sense of the word is not really needed. On the other hand, without the focus that you're used to in everyday life you may find it difficult to stay with the meditation.

Instead of an empty peaceful mind you'll find the thoughts crowding in, all demanding attention like a bunch of unruly children. Unlike children they can be safely ignored. Allow yourself to accept that the thoughts are there, but don't try to shut them down. Leave them alone and turn your attention back to the meditation.

You may also find that you start well, and then suddenly realize that you've drifted off mentally and have been deep in thought about something. This isn't a failure on your part, it's simply how meditation is sometimes. Gently bring your attention away from the subject of your thoughts and back to the meditation.

Use the space below to make notes about your attitude to concentration:

_____

_____

_____

_____

_____

→ # External distractions

However carefully you arrange your private meditation space you will be aware of distractions. Outside noises such as people in the street, traffic, children playing or even birdsong will filter through to your attention. By now it won't surprise you to learn that the mindful response is to acknowledge what you hear and gently bring your attention back to the meditation.

Use the space below to make notes about your attitude to distractions, and how you plan to approach this:

_____

_____

_____

_____

_____

→ Being on call

Sometimes of course the distraction is inside the home. You may hear loud music, the TV, people talking (or even arguing) and so on. Just as the people you live with will learn to leave you in peace while you meditate, so you will gradually learn that they can manage without you. It is not healthy for anyone to be on call 24/7, and even if you have demanding caring duties you will benefit from the short break that meditation brings, and be a better carer as a result.

Use the same technique of mentally acknowledging the distraction while gently returning your attention to the meditation. When you acknowledge you will doubtless also assess. Most distractions can be safely ignored, but you aren't being asked to ignore a scream of pain or the smell of burning.

If you've come to regard yourself as the lynchpin of your family group you may find it hard to let go in this way. Ask yourself what it says about your life if you can't find the time and privacy for a short meditation – everyone needs some down time. If you have particular concerns about time, use a timer to limit your sessions. Choose one with a gentle ring or bleep, and relax in the knowledge that you won't overrun.

Use the space below to make notes about your attitude to being on call, and how you plan to approach this:

_____

_____

_____

_____

_____

_____

→ Qualities needed for mindfulness and meditation

It must by now be apparent that there are certain mental qualities that contribute to a mindful approach. As well as the specific qualities of living in the moment, acceptance and detachment, there are other more generalized attitudes that feed into mindfulness. Some you may already have, some you may acquire along the way, but all will have a positive effect on your life and your happiness.

PATIENCE

Patience has already been mentioned. As well as being an important part of your approach to meditation, patience will help with everyday mindfulness. It's particularly helpful in relationships – it takes patience to be a good listener, to give the other person time to say what they need to say.

 *Exercise 40*

PATIENCE

First identify and list a few frequently occurring situations that you know you tend to make you impatient. This can be anything from traffic jams and bank queues to a child who is never ready for school on time.

_____

_____

_____

_____

_____

_____

Now choose one and decide that the next time it arises you will choose to be patient.

Afterwards, make a note of any differences you noticed.

_____

_____

_____

_____

_____

_____

AN OPEN MIND

Keeping an open mind means that you don't pre-judge people or situations. You approach each new experience with a fresh clean attitude, untainted by past experiences and preconceptions. It isn't a neutral quality. On the contrary, if your mind is open you'll be eager and interested in everything. The traditional way of describing this attitude is 'beginner's mind' – in other words, approach everything with the fresh interested attitude of a beginner.

 *Exercise 41*

OPENING YOUR MIND

First identify and list a few frequently occurring situations where you know you are inclined to prejudge. This is usually because you think you know what to expect – a certain person is always grumpy, or a certain task is always tedious.

_____

_____

_____

_____

_____

_____

Now choose one and decide that the next time it arises you will choose to keep an open mind. Afterwards, make a note of any differences you noticed.

_____

_____

_____

_____

_____

_____

WILLINGNESS TO BE VULNERABLE

Very often when people are defensive, with closed minds, it's because of the fear of change or newness. If you can let go of that fear you'll find that many difficulties suddenly disappear. Try deliberately asking yourself, 'How can this hurt me?' Almost always the answer will be, 'Not at all'. Sometimes the roots of defensiveness go back a long way, into your childhood, so letting go of it can be quite a challenge. Take your time and return to the exercise as often as you need to.

Exercise 42

BEING VULNERABLE

First identify and list a few frequently occurring situations where you know you tend to go on the defensive.

_____

_____

_____

_____

_____

_____

Now choose the least challenging one and decide that the next time it arises you will resist the urge to be defensive. (Later you may choose to work on other items on the list.)

Afterwards, make a note of any differences you noticed:

_____

_____

_____

_____

_____

_____

CURIOSITY

Once you let go of defensiveness and prejudging, it's easier to be genuinely curious. One advantage of detachment is that the emotional distance it gives you means it becomes easier to engage your interest.

For instance, if someone is rude to you, you may well react with knee-jerk irritation. If you can take a step back (that is, if you can detach a little) you might well find yourself thinking 'I wonder why they would do that?'

CURIOSITY

Using the lists you have already made, choose items where your curiosity is engaged. Note them below:

_____

_____

_____

_____

_____

_____

Ask yourself why other items on the list are not so engaging, and consider if you could extend your curiosity to all of them. Use the space below to make notes:

_____

_____

_____

_____

_____

_____

KINDNESS

Kindness is a key quality that underpins and informs all mindfulness. Being kind to yourself is the first step towards extending kindness to other people, indeed to the whole universe. Sometimes being kind to yourself can be the hardest thing of all, but that is where mindfulness starts. You will have days when you struggle to accept, to live in the moment, to detach. Times when you are impatient, or defensive, perhaps because you are tired or rushed. It's at these times that you most need to be kind to yourself. This is not the same as making excuses, in fact it involves accepting what has happened without excuses.

 Exercise 44

KINDNESS

Think of something that has happened recently where you aren't happy about your behaviour. Use your visualization technique to recreate the event, and be an observer of what happened. Watch yourself and allow yourself to feel a kindly forgiveness.

Use the space below to make notes about the experience of doing this:

_____

_____

_____

_____

_____

_____

→ Bringing it all together

As well as the three key qualities of living in the moment, acceptance and detachment, you've now looked at the various other aspects of mindfulness, including the basic quality of kindness. The process of bringing all this together into your individual experience of mindfulness will take time, and will grow gradually as you persevere with meditation and the other mindful practices. However, you can make a start with the following exercise. For once, instead of looking at, analysing and reliving difficult experiences, you are going to choose to enjoy yourself.

ALLOWING YOURSELF PLEASURE

Choose a gentle activity that you enjoy. For instance, craftwork, walking in a park or in the countryside, cooking, eating, or gardening. Choose a time when you can do it alone and undisturbed. Let go of all goals such as fitness (if you're walking) or weight loss (if you're cooking or eating). Enjoy the activity as mindfully as possible, by being entirely in the moment, accepting, detached and kindly. Savour every aspect of the experience. There is no need to make notes for this exercise.

→ Dealing with difficulties

TOO MUCH TO TAKE ON BOARD

Do you feel overwhelmed by the number of things you're being asked to change in order to be more mindful? Remember that it doesn't have to happen overnight, and indeed change that is slow and organic is often more lasting and solid than the speedy miracles beloved of reality TV. The most important thing is to understand that it is possible to change attitudes. They are changing all the time anyway, and if you look back you'll see that you're not the same person as you were 10 or 20 years ago. You can return to this chapter from time to time and repeat the exercises, working at a speed that suits you.

FEELING YOU'LL NEVER MANAGE IT

You may feel that you can't change your attitudes, that your attitudes are who you are. You already know that the mindful thing is to accept this about yourself, and, at this stage, you can just let it be. As you progress into mindfulness you will find yourself opening up to the possibility of change.

YOU'RE THE KIND OF PERSON THAT NEEDS GOALS

Perhaps your goal needs to be to let go of having goals. Try it, in small doses, and you'll gradually come to relish the peaceful break from being so driven.

BEING OPEN JUST MEANS PEOPLE TAKE ADVANTAGE

If your life so far has taught you to be self-protective, don't feel you have to let go of that all at once. Start by being open within yourself – open to the new concepts and practices of mindfulness.

Developing your skills

▶ Revisit the lists from each exercise and mark any items that you would like to continue to work on.

▶ Repeat any exercises that you feel the need to.

▶ Repeat Exercise 45 as often as you can.

What have I learnt?

→ What have you learnt about your mental qualities?

_____

_____

_____

_____

→ What have you learnt about treating yourself with kindness?

_____

_____

_____

_____

→ List any remaining concerns you have about meditation.

_____

_____

_____

_____

Where to next?

 You now know how you are going to organize your meditation sessions, and how you are going to approach them mentally. You can continue to fine-tune both aspects but at the same time you can get started on your practice – don't get caught in the trap of waiting till everything is perfectly in place. The practice itself will teach you what needs to be changed.

The next chapter will look at the three-minute breathing space, which is a simple mindfulness exercise that can be extremely beneficial in its own right as well as providing the basis for the next levels of practice.

6 Three-minute breathing space

In this chapter you will:

▶ learn about breathing spaces
▶ practise the three-minute breathing space
▶ learn how to use mindful breathing spaces.

A breathing space is anything that gives you a little break from what you are doing and sends you back refreshed to your task. Mostly we take breathing spaces by switching tasks. For instance, you might leave your desk to get a drink, or gaze out of the window while sending a personal text, and go back to work after five minutes or so. Motorway services are full of people enjoying breathing spaces – talking, eating, using the cash machine, making calls, shopping and so on.

Less often, breathing spaces are a chance to rest – you might see someone parked up asleep in their car, or sunbathing in the park during their lunch break. Anyone who is home-based knows how easy it is to watch a little daytime TV as a way of taking a break.

You probably don't think of any of these as 'breathing spaces' and may not be aware that, at regular intervals throughout the day, you find a reason to take a brief break.

YOUR TYPICAL BREATHING SPACES

Think about how you tend to take breathing spaces at work, at home and during leisure activities. Here are a few examples to get you started.

Work

Cigarette break

Morning drink

Chat with co-worker

_____

_____

_____

_____

Home

Cup of tea

TV

Read the paper

_____

_____

_____

_____

Leisure

Stop exercising to drink water

Lean on spade and think about planting plan

Coffee break during evening class

_____

_____

_____

_____

_____

Most breathing spaces are random and without structure, a few minutes snatched for yourself and used in whatever way is possible at the time. You may well find that you need more breathing spaces when doing something uncongenial compared with when you're enjoying yourself.

⏰ *Exercise 47*

ASSESS YOUR BREATHING SPACES

Look through your list of breathing spaces and ask yourself:

What do I need from a breathing space? Do these really work for me?

_____

_____

_____

_____

_____

_____

A mindful breathing space is designed to give you maximum benefit in a very short time. Rather than switching tasks or resting, you will give your full attention to yourself. If you're tired, it will refresh you, and if you're stressed it will help you calm down. If you're struggling to solve a problem the breathing space will clear your mind and you'll be able to return to the problem mentally refreshed.

You can take a mindful breathing space anywhere at any time, but remember to observe the simple precautions mentioned in Chapter 4:

▶ Consider the safety of others, for instance if you are responsible for supervising children, or operating machinery.

▶ Check out your personal safety, especially if you are in a public place. You can keep your eyes open if necessary while doing the exercise.

You will need to take a few preparatory steps:

▶ Stop whatever task you are engaged in; you will need your full attention.

▶ Make yourself as comfortable physically as possible, but don't get into a position for sleep.

▶ Remember to turn off your mobile phone.

→ Three-minute breathing space

A mindful breathing space has a specific three-part structure. Start by trying each of the three stages separately. You don't have to time yourself to exactly a minute, roughly a minute will do. Make notes after each stage – record how it felt, and any difficulties you encountered.

Set aside quiet time when you are on your own for doing the following exercises – this is practice so don't try to use the breathing space in real life yet. If you are under a lot of stress, or dealing with strong emotions, be aware that you may need extra time to work through the exercises. Stepping off the daily treadmill for even a short time can result in a rush of tiredness, or emotions welling up. Take it gently and allow plenty of time.

THE FIRST MINUTE

Spend the first minute checking yourself out, giving your full awareness to yourself and your current state. Don't worry about or judge anything you notice, just observe. Remember you are only giving yourself one minute for checking so there isn't time for analysis or brooding.

CHECKING

Sit quietly and focus your attention as follows:

▶ **Breathing.** Briefly pay attention to your breathing. Don't try to change or control it.

▶ Check your body, observe both pleasant sensations and any discomfort. Try to accept both equally.

▶ Now look at your thoughts, all the many things that are probably on your mind at the moment. No need to list each one, just try to let go of all of them.

▶ Move on to your emotions, observe what you are feeling and accept it.

Use the space below to make notes:

_____

_____

_____

_____

_____

_____

THE SECOND MINUTE

During the second minute you focus entirely on your breathing, without trying to change or control it. For just one minute you can ignore everything else – your mind, the rest of your body, your emotions. Breathe and engage fully with the sensations and process of breathing.

 Exercise 49

BREATHING

Sit quietly and focus your attention as follows:

▶ Give your full attention to your breathing and especially the way your stomach moves when you breathe in and out.

▶ Let go of any thoughts, emotions and physical sensations – this takes practice and will be easier some days than others.

▶ By focussing on your breathing and letting go of everything else, you will narrow your awareness down to just one thing.

Use the space below to make notes:

_____

_____

_____

_____

_____

_____

_____

_____

_____

THE THIRD MINUTE

The third minute is very similar to the first, but without the checking element – you take your awareness back into your body, then into your thoughts, and finally into your emotions. It can help if you think of your awareness travelling gently back as you breathe, each breath taking you further into your body, your thoughts and your emotions.

 **Exercise 50**

EXPANDING AWARENESS

Sit quietly and focus your attention as follows:

▶ Allow your awareness to move into your body.
▶ Next allow your awareness to move into your thinking mind.
▶ Finally allow your awareness to move into your emotions.

Use the space below to make notes:

_____

_____

_____

_____

_____

_____

_____

_____

_____

→ Putting it all together

Now that you've tried each of the three stages it's time to put them all together. If you look at the three stages you'll see that there's a progression:

▶ **Checking**: being aware of what's going on for you at that moment, physically, mentally and emotionally, without judging or engaging.

▶ **Breathing**: letting go of everything you noticed during the first minute and concentrating your entire awareness on your breathing.

▶ **Expanding**: taking your awareness back into yourself.

 *Exercise 51*

CHECKING, BREATHING, EXPANDING

Try a complete three-minute breathing space and see how it feels for you. If it helps you to remember, tell yourself 'CBE' (for Checking, Breathing, Expanding).

Use the space below to make notes:

_____

_____

_____

_____

_____

_____

If you think about it, you've been on a short journey away from yourself and back again. During the first minute you acknowledged everything you were thinking and feeling (both physically and emotionally) and decided to let go. The second minute of nothing but breathing created a space where the letting go could happen. During the third minute you were able to return into yourself calmer and a little detached from the strains and stresses of your day.

Three minutes is a suitable timescale for a mindful breathing space, but the more you practise it the more you'll be able to play with the timing. You may decide to spend longer over it when you have the chance, or if you're really pressed you may condense it right down to the space of three breaths, one for each element.

The important thing is to follow the progression. There may be one stage that you can't see the point of, or don't find very easy, but stick with it and do all three.

▶ If you omit the first minute and fail to check round yourself you'll find it very difficult to let go during the breathing stage – any physical sensations, thoughts or feelings will be clamouring for your attention, rather like children that feel they've been ignored.

▶ If you omit the breathing stage you won't achieve a helpful level of detachment.

▶ And if you omit the final stage you won't get the benefit of feeling calmer and more refreshed.

Don't judge yourself if you feel you haven't done it right – there is no success or failure, it's enough that you tried. If, despite your best efforts, the thoughts, worries and emotions came crowding in on you during the second minute you will still have gained some benefit from taking the short break.

→ Using the three-minute breathing space

Once you have tried each of the three stages and put them together you can look at ways the three-minute breathing space can help you in your everyday life.

REVIST YOUR BREATHING SPACES

Have a look at the list of your personal breathing spaces you made in Exercise 46 and see if there's a pattern to when you take them. Perhaps you always close your eyes for a minute on the train home, or you like to have a quick coffee after finishing a supermarket shop. Perhaps you needed a moment to yourself after a stressful meeting, or after a day spent with a fretful baby.

Work

Cigarette break – when emails get tedious

Morning drink – need an energy boost

Chat with co-worker – welcome distraction

_____

_____

_____

_____

_____

Home

Cup of tea – before facing the washing up

TV – too tired for anything else

Read the paper – helps me switch off after work

_____

_____

_____

_____

_____

Leisure

Stop exercising to drink water – getting my breath back!

Lean on spade and think about planting plan – eases my stiff back

Coffee break during evening class – good to socialize with the other students

_____

_____

_____

_____

_____

You'll probably see that there are some regular times when you take a breathing space, and some that occur unexpectedly due to the pressures of your day. You can choose to use the mindful three-minute breathing space for both types.

➜ Formal breathing spaces

Make a conscious decision to programme three-minute breathing spaces into fixed times in your schedule. For example, you might use a breathing space:

▶ for the first three minutes of your lunch break

▶ just before your children are due home from school

▶ immediately before you give a presentation.

The process of the breathing space will help you clear your mind of one set of concerns, ready to focus on the next set.

Exercise 53

FORMAL BREATHING SPACES

Make a list of times when it would be helpful for you to take a formal breathing space:

_____

_____

_____

_____

_____

_____

_____

_____

_____

_____

→ Informal breathing spaces

You can also use breathing spaces informally, as the need arises. You may find this easier after you've established the habit of using them formally. You'll start to recognize the times when you unexpectedly need to clear your head or calm yourself. If possible, take the full three minutes to step back from what's going on, but remember that even the space three breaths is enough to create some benefit.

In really extreme circumstances, perhaps in the middle of an argument, you can take a breathing space as the event happens, perhaps while the other person is talking. This isn't ideal, but it will have a similar effect to the traditional advice to 'count to ten' and may stop things escalating.

→ Benefits of the three-minute breathing space

TRANSITION

Use a three-minute breathing space when switching between different types of task or different parts of your day. It will help you let go of one set of concerns and approach the next set with a fresh mind.

COMING OUT OF AUTOPILOT

A breathing space is a simple way to spend a little time living in the moment.

GOING INTO BEING MODE

It will help you accustom yourself to Being mode.

INCREASED UNDERSTANDING OF YOURSELF

If you regularly take a step back from your busy day and check in with yourself, you'll start to achieve greater insights.

SENSE OF PERSPECTIVE

A few moments of detachment will help you see things in perspective, rather than letting small worries loom too large.

CLEARER THINKING

By clearing your mind you'll find creative thinking is easier and solutions to problems come to mind unbidden.

PRACTISING DETACHMENT

Detachment is an unfamiliar concept to many of us, and a mindful breathing space helps you become more comfortable with it.

EASING YOURSELF INTO MINDFULNESS

Overall the breathing space exercise sets you on the road to more mindful living.

→ Dealing with difficulties

PROBLEMS RE-ENGAGING

You may worry that it will be difficult to pick up the reins of your busy day once you've taken a short break from it. It's true that a three-minute breathing space is more of a complete break than say a cup of coffee and five minutes with the crossword. It is more likely that you will go back to your day refreshed and reinvigorated, but you will only find out by trying it. Start with times when it won't matter too much if you are slow to get going again and learn what works for you.

EMOTIONAL OVERLOAD

As already explained, you need to test out the effects of the breathing space in a safe way when you are alone and private. The technique is very useful during stressful times but only if you have already familiarized yourself with it, so don't push yourself if you are already dealing with a crisis.

Developing your skills

▶ Revisit the list from Exercise 46 and continue to assess which of your personal breathing spaces could be changed for mindful breathing spaces.

▶ Repeat the exercises until you feel comfortable with the concept and practice of a three-minute breathing space.

▶ As you learn more about how this works for you, you can start to use mindful breathing spaces in real life, as events happen. Don't rush this.

What have I learnt?

→ What have you learnt about the kinds of breathing spaces you take?

_____

_____

_____

_____

_____

→ What have you learnt about how helpful or otherwise your personal breathing spaces are to you?

_____

_____

_____

_____

_____

→ What have you learnt about mindful breathing spaces?

_____

_____

_____

_____

_____

Where to next?

 The three-minute breathing space is an important step towards mindfulness so take your time getting used to it. Although it's a small exercise in terms of time, it's big in terms of accustoming you to how mindfulness feels, and how it can help.

When you're ready move on to the next chapter, which will take your new skills and move them on to an entirely different type of exercise – the body scan. A body scan takes longer than a breathing space and takes you further into mindfulness.

7 Body scan

In this chapter you will learn:
▶ about your relationship with your body
▶ how to do a body scan
▶ about the benefits of a body scan.

 Remember: do not use the exercises in this chapter as a substitute for seeing your doctor about a physical problem.

Yet another disadvantage of living on autopilot is the problem of losing touch with your body. Even if you are the kind of person who goes to the gym you will probably listen to music while exercising rather than listen to your body. And yet your body is a vital part of who you are, since you can only interact with the external world through your bodily senses. There are more than five of these – as well as sight, hearing, touch, taste and smell there are senses such as balance, orientation and proprioception (your sense of where your limbs are in space). And when the external world triggers an emotional response in you, your body will feel that too.

Exercise 54

EMOTIONS AND YOUR BODY

Where in your body do you feel anger?

_____

Where do you feel fear?

_____

Where do you feel happiness?

_____

Where do you feel sadness?

_____

Where do you feel anticipation?

_____

Where do you feel well-being?

_____

It's quite common to feel emotions in the throat, chest and stomach, but each person will have their own set of responses. Some people feel sick with anger, others shake all over. Your life experiences can affect your response too. Fear may produce a sudden stab of pain in the ankle where a scary dog bit you many years ago, or sadness may twinge your neck because you once missed a party due to having mumps.

Emotions can be stored in your body too, in the muscles and organs. This only seems to relate to deep-seated emotions such as grief, and may be connected with repression. If something is too much for you to feel at the time, you may hold it back and since it has to go somewhere your body takes up the slack for you. People who work with the body, such as physiotherapists and masseurs, occasionally have clients who start to cry during a treatment, because a stored emotion has inadvertently been released (this almost always comes as a relief).

Most of us are unaware of physical reactions to emotions, although they can often be the source of bodily discomfort. All emotions produce physiological changes – for instance, increased heart rate or changes in blood pressure, and these will have an effect on your sense of physical well-being. For instance, if you feel anxiety in your stomach then an ongoing worry may well produce acid indigestion or a continuous feeling of mild nausea.

 *Exercise 55*

FINDING THE CONNECTIONS

In the first column below, make a list of any minor discomforts that you are living with at the moment, such as backache or indigestion. Do any of them relate to the parts of the body where you feel specific emotions? Use the second column to list any possible connections.

Type of discomfort	Possible emotional connection
_____	_____
_____	_____
_____	_____
_____	_____
_____	_____
_____	_____
_____	_____
_____	_____
_____	_____
_____	_____

You may have already experienced an emotional release during the exercises you have done. While this is fairly common, it is by no means universal and you may practise mindfulness for years without experiencing it. On the other hand, everyone will experience the emotions of the moment while engaged in a breathing space, body scan or meditation, simply because emotions that are easy to ignore when you're busy become noticeable when you are quiet.

In Chapter 3 you practised breathing into an emotion. Now you can extend that to explore the connection between your emotions and your physical sensations, soothing any discomfort.

 *Exercise 56*

BREATHING INTO DISCOMFORT

Choose an item from your list where there may possibly be a connection between minor discomfort and an emotion.

▶ Sit or lie quietly and focus on your breathing. Observe the change from breathing in to breathing out, feel your lungs filling and emptying, feel your stomach moving as you breathe.

▶ Now turn your attention to the part of your body where you feel the discomfort. Allow yourself to feel it without judging or worrying about it.

▶ As you breathe in, encourage yourself to feel you are sending the breath into that part of your body. As you breathe out, allow yourself to feel the breath gently taking the discomfort away.

▶ Also allow yourself to feel any emotions that arise during the exercise, again without judging.

▶ Send soothing breath into the emotion, and allow cleansing breath to leave it.

▶ When you are ready, allow yourself to gently emerge from the exercise and reconnect with your everyday life.

Use the space below to make notes about the experience.

Ask yourself:

Did the physical discomfort change during the exercise?

In what way did it change?

Did any emotions arise during the exercise?

What emotions did you experience?

How intense were they?

Did the emotions change during the exercise?

In what way did they change?

_____

_____

_____

_____

_____

_____

_____

_____

_____

This exercise is a small preparation for a full body scan. During a body scan you focus very much on the physical aspects of what you are feeling in your body, but since emotions may well arise, the exercise prepares you for this. It is unlikely that the emotions will be overwhelming, but remember that at any time you can decide to come out of the exercise. Always allow time for reconnecting with your world.

→ Body scan

During a body scan you will relax, breathe and move your attention and awareness round your body in a set order. It's important to stick to the order rather than rush your attention to the site of any discomfort. You can always repeat Exercise 56 if you want to focus on soothing discomfort, and in any case you will come to those places eventually and you will be able to breathe into them and soothe them if you wish. During a body scan you will note any sensations without judging. This is not the time for thoughts like, 'I really need to lose some weight' or, 'I hope that twinge doesn't mean I'll need a hip replacement'. In fact, it's best to suspend thinking as far as possible. Let your mind be blank and open so that you are able to focus fully on your breathing and your body and nothing else.

Remember to organize yourself so that you are private, safe, comfortable and warm during the body scan. Turn off your phone if possible, lean back or lie down, and close your eyes.

BODY SCAN

Allow plenty of time for your first full body scan. Read through the instructions before you start. If your concentration lapses, gently bring your focus back to the exercise.

▶ Spend a little time focussing on your breathing. Don't judge, just observe. Notice any changes – perhaps your breathing will quieten once you are physically relaxed, perhaps not.

▶ Take stock of your body in a general way. Feel the weight of it against the chair or bed, feel the textures of clothing or covers, any draught on the skin of your face, any discomfort.

► Focus your awareness on the big toe of your left foot. Mentally allow your next inbreath to travel down to that toe. If it helps, imagine the life-giving oxygen in your breath reaching the toe, and the waste gases leaving the toe as you breathe out. Maintain your awareness in the toe even when you breathe out, for as many breaths as you wish.

► Keep your awareness in just that toe. Feel any sensations, whether it is warm or cold, stiff or relaxed, touching the next toe or touching clothing. Remember not to judge – you may have a bunion, or callouses, you may think your toes are ugly, but right now this is just your left big toe.

► When you are ready move on, taking your awareness to the next toe along. Repeat the process, breathing into the toe on an inbreath, keeping your awareness there when you breathe out, noticing without judging.

► Without rushing work your way round your entire body, in the following order: all the toes of the left foot one at a time, the instep, heel and ankle. Move up into your calf and shin, your knee, and your thigh. Move across your pelvis and down into the big toe of your right foot. Repeat the sequence of individual toes, instep, heel, ankle, calf, shin, knee and thigh.

► Take your awareness into your pelvis then hips, buttocks and genitals. As well as being a sensitive area, this is likely to give rise to judgemental thoughts about your sexual attractiveness, habits or relationships. This is not the time for them, so let go.

► Take your awareness to your stomach, feel it moving as you breathe. If emotions arise, allow yourself to feel them without judging, blaming, explaining or defending. Be gently interested and breathe into the emotions.

► Move on to your chest and throat and continue to be aware of internal and external sensations as well as any emotions.

► When you reach your head and face, take extra time for this complicated area. Start with the muscles of your face and jaw, and then take your awareness into your eyes, nose, mouth and ears. Move up to your forehead, over the top of your head and down into the back of your neck and into your shoulders.

► Take your awareness into your left thumb followed by each finger, the palm and back of your hand, wrist, forearm, elbow and upper arm. Repeat with the right hand and arm, starting with the thumb.

► From your right shoulder move your awareness slowly down your spine until you reach the small of your back.

► Now imagine your awareness spreading slowly and calmly from the small of your back through your entire body. If it helps, imagine soothing warmth emanating from your back into all parts of your body. With each inward breath expand your awareness a little further into your body. Relish the sensation of harmony between your mind and your body, breathing together.

► Now you can forget about mindfulness and the requirements of the body scan. Allow yourself to be carried by the rhythm of your breathing. Allow yourself to float.

► When you are ready, open your eyes. Take a few moments to return to full awareness of the outside world.

Use the space below to record the experience. Ask yourself:

Was I able to give full attention to each part of my body?

Did my mind wander during the exercise? Was I able to gently return my mind to the exercise?

Did any emotions arise during the exercise?

What emotions did I experience?

How intense were they?

Did the emotions change during the exercise?

In what way did they change?

_____

_____

_____

_____

_____

_____

_____

_____

_____

_____

....

➜ Benefits of body scan

RELAXATION

Although a body scan is not a relaxation exercise, it will often have the side-effect of inducing physical relaxation, with all its attendant benefits. Unnecessary muscle tension can make you much more tired than you need to be, so relaxing for a short time can free up energy.

WELL-BEING

The combination of physical relaxation and clearing your mind while you focus on the body scan will often leave you with a peaceful feeling of well-being. This won't happen every time, but when it does, enjoy it as an added bonus.

IMPROVED RELATIONSHIP WITH YOUR BODY

If you do a body scan regularly you will achieve a better understanding of your body and how it functions. Instead of regarding it as something separate from who you are, you'll integrate your mind and body into an harmonious whole.

MORE BEING

Just like the three-minute breathing space, a body scan allows you to experience Being mode in an easy non-challenging way.

LEARNING TO WORK WITH YOUR ATTENTION

The body scan takes the short experience of the three-minute breathing space, where you move quickly from a general focus to a narrow focus and back to the general, and expands it. You start with a general awareness of your body, spend quite a long time with a narrow focus on each part, and then move out to a general awareness again. It gives you just enough of a task to help you stay focussed. This is all good practice towards meditation, in which the lack of structure can be disconcerting at first.

EMOTIONAL RELEASE

Emotional release can seem worrying but this is largely because it is unfamiliar. Once freed of the burden of stored emotions, your body will feel lighter and you'll have more energy.

EMOTIONAL AND MENTAL SENSITIVITY

As welling as learning more about your body, you'll become more sensitive to the signals it sends you about your emotional and mental health.

→ Dealing with difficulties

FALLING ASLEEP

The relaxation benefit of a body scan can easily tip over into falling asleep. While you may need the sleep, you will have missed out on the body scan practice. If it happens repeatedly you'll need to look at your sleep as you probably aren't getting enough. Avoid doing the body scan at times when you know you'll be tired, and if you are worried that you will sleep for too long then set an alarm or timer, preferably one with a gentle tone.

THOUGHTS CROWDING IN

It's quite common to find that, as soon as you take the time out of your busy day and sit or lie comfortably to try a body scan, your mind starts racing. There are a hundred and one things demanding your attention, phone calls to make, chores to remember, and your busy brain wants you to attend to them now. If this is a pattern with you then make a conscious decision before you start that you will leave everything to one side for the duration of the exercise. Then when the thoughts appear you already have permission from yourself to ignore them.

MIND WANDERING

It's equally common to start well, focussing on breathing and body, and then suddenly realize with a start that your mind has wandered off and that for some time you've been lying back comfortably thinking about Christmas, holidays or some treat you've promised yourself. If your life is very stressful your mind might also wander less happily into your worries. In both cases gently remind yourself that this time was set aside for the body scan, and bring your attention back. Don't judge yourself over this, everybody's mind wanders sometimes.

PAIN

If you are struggling with physical pain you may find the body scan difficult initially for two reasons. It may increase your focus on the painful part that you are trying to ignore, and you may find it hard to take your awareness to other parts of your body. Don't give up, but take it slowly. Try breaking the body scan down into short sections while you are learning how it works for you and keep to the prescribed order for working round your body. You can also set up a separate exercise for the painful areas.

Exercise 58

SOOTHING PAIN

▶ Sit or lie as comfortably as you can. Spend a little time focussing on your breathing. Don't judge, just observe.

▶ Take stock of your body in a general way. Feel the weight of it against the chair or bed, feel the textures of clothing or covers, any draught on the skin of your face, any discomfort.

▶ Take your awareness to the painful area. As you breathe in, imagine the breathe travelling to that area, soothing and warming it. As you breathe out, imagine the pain leaving as the breath leaves.

▶ Take your awareness into the surrounding areas. They may well be tense, so allow yourself to gently let go of the tension.

▶ Take your awareness into your whole body and allow yourself to relax.

▶ When you are ready, gently emerge from the exercise and allow time to reconnect with your life.

Developing your skills

▶ Revisit the list from Exercise 54 and, based on what you've learnt from your initial body scan, fine-tune your understanding of where in your body you feel your emotions.

▶ Continue to do the exercises.

▶ While there is no need for a regular commitment, you might like to programme body scan sessions into your week. You could, for instance, do a body scan at the end of your working week and another one at the beginning of the next working week.

What have I learnt?

→ What have you learnt about how your emotions are expressed physically?

_____

_____

_____

_____

_____

→ What have you learnt about emotional release?

_____

_____

_____

_____

_____

→ What changes have you observed as a result of practising the body scan?

_____

_____

_____

_____

_____

Where to next?

 Regular body scans will take you a long way towards mindful living. You will learn to come out of autopilot and engage with your body in a peaceful and non-judgemental way, acknowledging and accepting it as it is. Combined with a healthy level of detachment (rather than obsessing about physical flaws), this will set you on the road to mindfulness. You will also find that your experience of the three-minute breathing space is subtly changed the more you explore the body scan – your greater familiarity with yourself, and the way you experience your emotions, will make the breathing space easier and help you move more deeply into yourself in a short time.

You now have a good basic grounding in mindfulness, and in the next chapter you will start to explore meditation. However, take as long as you need to feel comfortable with the full body scan before moving on.

8 Breathing meditation

....

In this chapter you will learn:
▶ to start meditating
▶ to deal with difficulties
▶ to persevere.

....

Before you move on to your first sitting meditation, think back over what you've already learnt. If there are any significant gaps, anything you've rushed or skipped or attempted but struggled with, go back and re-read that part, and repeat the exercises. The exercise below will help you decide if there is anything you would benefit from repeating. Remember that mindfulness is a journey with no timetable and no estimated time of arrival.

Exercise 59

REVIEW

Consider the following points and ask yourself if you feel you've achieved some understanding of each one. You're not aiming for perfection here, just a degree of insight, and an acceptable level of comfort with new concepts and practices.

▶ **Coming out of autopilot.** Can you feel the difference between autopilot and living in the moment? Are you trying to come out of autopilot for at least part of every day?

▶ **Going into Being mode.** Can you feel the difference between Being and Doing modes? Are you taking time every day to just Be?

▶ **Acknowledging.** Do you now acknowledge difficult issues, or are you in denial? (Remember that no one else needs to know about this.)

▶ **Accepting.** How far are you able to accept without judging or rushing to change things? (Remember that change will be possible, but acceptance is the first step).

▶ **Detachment.** Are you able to stand back from your experiences and observe your reactions? Can you resist the urge to engage?

▶ **Time.** Have you looked at your life and decided where meditation will fit in? Have you looked at how this will affect other people?

▶ **Place:** Do you have a quiet, warm, private space for meditation?

▶ **Posture:** Have you chosen your posture and practised it?

▶ **Boredom:** Do you expect to be bored and fidgety, or have you opened your mind to the idea that meditation could be interesting in itself?

▶ **Physical discomfort:** Are you ready to cope with minor physical discomfort?

▶ **Letting go of goals:** Are you able to let go of the striving goal-driven mindset while you are being mindful?

▶ **Establishing a routine:** Do you accept the value of a routine for meditation, or are you still hoping to squeeze it in as and when you can?

▶ **Concentration:** Is your mind like a butterfly, or have you begun to achieve concentration? (Regular practice of the three-minute breathing space and the body scan will help with this).

▶ **Distractions:** Have you thought about the type of external distractions you're likely to encounter? Do you feel able to ignore them?

▶ **On call:** Have you made practical arrangements so that you won't be on call during your meditation sessions, and do you feel able to mentally let go of being on call?

▶ **Patience:** Are you ready to approach meditation patiently, without expecting instant results?

▶ **An open mind:** Are you beginning to open your mind to the new concepts and experiences of mindfulness?

- **Vulnerability:** Can you cope with feeling vulnerable?
- **Curiosity:** Have you engaged with the process of mindfulness and are you curious about it?
- **Emotional release:** Have you experienced emotional release and were you able to cope with it? If you haven't experienced it, do you have any worries about it?
- **Kindness:** Are you able to feel kindly towards yourself, and any difficulties you may be encountering? Do you judge and criticize yourself or are you now beginning to treat yourself with kindness?
- **Everyday mindfulness:** How far have you already absorbed mindfulness into your daily life? Bear in mind there is no timetable for this and everyone is different.

Use the space below to make notes about anything you'd like to revisit before starting on meditation.

_____

_____

_____

_____

_____

_____

_____

_____

It's important to understand that mindful meditation is not the same as a visualization, body scan or three-minute breathing space. With visualization your mind is very active, re-creating an event in great detail, and you are trying to be fully engaged with the re-creation. A body scan focusses your attention on different parts of your body, and your mind is fully engaged with that. A three-minute breathing space also requires mental focus which moves your attention from broad to narrow and back again. In meditation your mind is tranquil, untroubled by thoughts and emotions, and your only focus is on your breathing.

To help ease the transition into full meditation, repeat Exercise 38 from Chapter 4:

 *Exercise 60*

REPEAT PRACTICE SESSION

Spend a few minutes sitting quietly in your chosen place, in your chosen posture, with eyes half closed and your gaze unfocussed. Don't try to meditate, just explore how it feels to sit like this. If you find yourself drawn into visualization, body scan or breathing space, gently take your attention away.

The next exercise is your first meditation. Before you do it, here are a few tips and reminders.

▶ Keep it short, as little as five to ten minutes for your first meditation.

▶ Choose a time and stick to it. Intention is important in mindfulness, and even a short meditation benefits from the clarity of an intention that you keep to.

▶ Even though it is short, it's important to go with your chosen routines for place and posture.

Exercise 61

FIRST MEDITATION

At your chosen time, go to your chosen place, make sure you are warm enough, not hungry or thirsty, and sit quietly in your preferred posture. Allow your eyes to half close and observe your breathing. Don't try to change it, although it will probably quieten as you sit. Bring your whole attention to your breathing. There is a lot to observe – parts of your body move as you breathe, there are different sensations as the air moves in and out of your nostrils and in and out of your chest, your diaphragm and stomach will feel different with each breath and so on. Allow yourself to experience the sensations without thoughts. You don't need to find the words to describe what you feel, you only need to feel it. If any thoughts appear in your mind, rather than grabbing hold of them, allow them to drift away.

After a few minutes, open your eyes fully and gradually leave the meditation.

Use the space below to make notes about the experience:

_____

_____

_____

_____

_____

_____

Whatever your experience of this short meditation, it is personal to you and entirely valid – it's not a question of success or failure. You may have instantly moved into a tranquil thought-free mental space and feel ready to meditate for longer, or you may have felt like you were just sitting still to no purpose. Your mind may have cleared of thoughts, or thoughts on many topics may have rushed busily into your mind. You may have felt nothing, emotionally, or your emotions may have kicked off big time.

If you were unfortunate enough to experience something unpleasant, that doesn't mean meditation is not for you. Take as much time as you need to settle yourself, and then give some thought to what happened. If, for instance, your life is stressful at the moment, the quietness of the meditation may have allowed the stress to well up. Equally, unresolved issues from the past may have emerged. Consider the various ways that you can look after yourself – you may need anything from a good night's sleep to sessions with a counsellor or therapist. Many people do find meditation helpful, so continue with the exercises while treating yourself gently.

Meditation: tips and hints

Now that you've had a small experience of meditation you can start to fine-tune your approach. Don't try to address everything at once. Instead, each time you repeat the short meditation exercise consider one aspect of your experience. Here are some suggestions:

▶ Forget about 'I must', 'I should', or 'I ought to' while you are meditating. Think of meditation as a holiday from all the concerns that usually drive you. It's time that you give to yourself and you can let go of feelings of guilt or inadequacy.

▶ Give the process a chance. Aim for eight weeks of daily sessions. This is long enough for you to really get a feel for meditation and find out if it is for you. If you miss the occasional session don't worry about it. After all, life is complicated for all of us. However, if you miss a lot of sessions revisit Chapter 4 and work through the planning stages again.

▶ Make your sessions as pleasant as possible. Don't let meditation become a burden. Create the atmosphere that you need to feel calm and peaceful, so that you look forward to the chance to take time out.

▶ If the time passes too slowly, try to let go of your awareness of time passing. Narrow your focus onto just the next breath. Allow yourself to be absorbed in the awareness of that one breath.

▶ Aim to meditate every day. Regularity is important in meditation, and establishing a routine of daily short meditations is more beneficial than occasional longer sessions. It's easy to slip into thinking that a long session has more point and that it's worth the preparation time, but actually the opposite is true.

Exercise 62

REGULAR MEDITATION

Repeat your short meditation exercise every day at the time you have allocated for that day, depending on your schedule. Although it is only a few minutes, put your full routine in place each time. If you feel the desire to meditate for longer then add a few minutes, but don't, at this stage, undertake long sessions.

Remember the routine: at your chosen time, go to your chosen place, make sure you are warm enough, not hungry or thirsty, and sit quietly in your preferred posture. Allow your eyes to half close and observe your breathing. Bring your whole attention to your breathing. You don't need to find the words to describe what you feel, you only need to feel it. If any thoughts appear in your mind, rather than grabbing hold of them, allow them to drift away.

After a few minutes, open your eyes fully and gradually leave the meditation.

→ Benefits of meditation

Many claims are made for meditation, and individuals benefit in many different ways. For this reason, as with all mindfulness, it's best to clear your mind of all expectations. Each meditation session will be different, bringing different benefits, and your practice will also have cumulative effects.

BREATHING

Although you will only observe your breathing and won't deliberately try to change it, you will often find that as the session progresses your breathing changes of its own accord, becoming calmer, slower and deeper. When this happens you will benefit both physically and mentally.

WELL-BEING

Some sessions will leave you with a peaceful feeling of well-being. This won't happen every time, but when it does, enjoy it as an added bonus.

MORE BEING

Meditation is the ultimate experience of Being. As your sessions become longer you will increasingly benefit from the break from Doing. Being will be increasingly integrated into your life, and as a result you'll be more energized and effective when you are in Doing mode.

INCREASED INSIGHT

You'll achieve greater insight into yourself and over time that will lead you into greater understanding and empathy with other people. You'll start to understand your own responses and take responsibility for them. You'll be more forgiving both of yourself and others.

EMOTIONAL HEALTH

Meditation will provide the space to feel your emotions and let them move on, as opposed to repressing them or clinging on to them. You'll find it easier to acknowledge and accept painful emotions and you'll become more emotionally stable.

CLEARER THINKING

Meditation allows your thinking mind to take a break and rest itself. Like a muscle, your mind will grow and strengthen during the rest period.

IMPROVED MENTAL HEALTH

Many people find that meditation gives them greater stability, reducing depression, phobias and anxiety.

GREATER WILL-POWER AND SELF-DISCIPLINE

Regular meditation requires will-power, not only to stick to your decision to meditate but also during the sessions, as you resist the urge to give up if it isn't going well or aren't in the mood on that particular day. At the same time the non-judgemental aspect of mindfulness means that the energy you used to put into negative self-criticism is freed up, making it more likely that you meet your commitment to daily meditation.

Exercise 63

CONSIDERING THE BENEFITS

Look through the list of benefits and decide how you feel about each one. Use the space below to make notes:

_____

_____

_____

_____

_____

_____

_____

_____

_____

_____

Are there any items that you are particularly focussed on, perhaps yearning for? Take a little time to think about this, and steel yourself to let go of the longing. Meditation brings benefits, but they aren't always the ones you wanted or expected, so come to it with an open mind. Let go of the wanting, and allow the benefits to appear in their own time.

→ Dealing with difficulties

STRANGE SENSATIONS

Some people occasionally experience strange sensations during a meditation session – twitching, feeling hot or cold, sweating, shivering, tingling and so on. Light can seem excessively bright, and you can feel slightly disorientated. If there is anything that you don't like, make a conscious decision to gently come out of the meditation. Try to avoid a panicky quick exit, which will only reinforce the discomfort. Allow the sensations to die down naturally – this usually happens very quickly.

WANTING TOO MUCH

If you've gone into meditation expecting an instant fix, or you've read accounts of other people being transformed by meditating, you may find you are disappointed in your first few sessions. It is very rare for anyone to experience immediate deep change. Meditation is a gradual, cumulative process, so let go of wanting and allow yourself to enjoy the process.

TOO TIRED

Even with good posture and eyes half open you may find yourself falling asleep. If you aren't getting enough sleep then look at how you can improve matters. Also, look at the time you've chosen for meditation. Is it your natural rhythm to be tired at that point of the day? Is it too close to a heavy meal, which encourages sleepiness?

NOT RELAXED

It may be that your first meditation sessions are too short to allow you to wind down, and yet it is too soon to attempt longer sessions. The answer is to take a little time to relax beforehand, and count that time as part of your meditation. You could, for instance, have a bath for half an hour and then meditate for ten minutes. Sitting down with a drink (not caffeinated) or listening to relaxing music are other ways of easing yourself into a quieter frame of mind. Eventually you will not need to relax first, and will spend the whole of the allocated time meditating.

TOO MANY THOUGHTS

Ironically at the very time that you choose to empty your mind for meditation you'll probably find that the thoughts come crowding in, possibly even more wildly and chaotically than usual. In fact your thoughts haven't changed, but the quiet space that you've started to create has allowed them room to run riot. Also you are noticing the contrast between your new quiet Self and the noisy thoughts. Remind yourself that you are giving your mind a break which will do it good. Try not to engage with the thoughts, and gradually they will quieten.

TOO JUDGEMENTAL

If your first session didn't go as expected, or you tend to see yourself as a failure, or you set yourself unrealistic goals, then you may be tempted to give up on meditation before you've even started. Remember it takes about eight weeks of regular meditation practice before you can really get a feel for it. Tell yourself that you made a commitment and you are going to stick to it.

DEALING WITH DIFFICULTIES

Look through the list of difficulties and decide how far you have experienced each one or if you have experienced it at all. Use the space below to make notes:

_____

_____

_____

_____

_____

_____

_____

_____

_____

_____

Spend a little time thinking about any difficulties that particularly bother you, or daunt you. Are you going to let them stop you meditating? Take steps as far as possible to minimize your difficulties, and then leave them alone. You've acknowledged them, now accept them and carry on with your meditation.

Developing your skills

▶ Revisit the list in Exercise 59 and work on any outstanding items.

▶ Make sure you meditate every day.

▶ Allow the length of time for sessions to increase gradually until you are meditating for 30 to 45 minutes every day. Take your time over this. If you overload yourself with long meditation sessions at the beginning you'll be more likely to feel overwhelmed and give up on meditating.

▶ Continue with body scans and three-minute breathing spaces.

What have I learnt?

→ What have you learnt about your preparation for meditation?

_____

_____

_____

_____

_____

→ What have you learnt from your first meditation session?

_____

_____

_____

_____

_____

→ What have you learnt about benefits and difficulties?

_____

_____

_____

_____

_____

_____

Where to next?

You've just taken an enormous step into full mindful meditation. Even with all the careful preparation and practice of other types of mindful exercise you may well have found this daunting. So well done. You may well feel that you need to focus on establishing your meditation practice, and there's nothing wrong with that. By all means set the book to one side while you do that.

If you choose to carry on, the next chapter introduces you to an entirely different aspect of mindfulness, mindful movement. You can choose to explore this while continuing with your meditation sessions or you can return to it when you are ready. Mindful movement is an extension of the mindful approach, asking you to fully engage with your body as it moves, both during tasks and during specific mindful movement exercises.

(9) *Mindful movement*

In this chapter you will learn:
▶ about informal mindful movement
▶ about formal mindful movement
▶ about mindfulness and fitness.

 Remember: don't pursue any exercises in this chapter that are too tough for you. Check with your doctor first if you have physical health problems.

Sitting meditation requires you to be physically still, but mindfulness as a general principle can be brought to everything you do, even the apparently simple acts of stretching or walking. Now that you have experienced repeated body scans you'll be starting to be more aware of your body at all times, and mindful movement takes that awareness a stage further.

Use the checklist in the following exercise to further explore your relationship with your body.

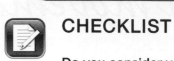 Exercise 65

CHECKLIST

Do you consider yourself to be generally active or inactive? ☐

Are you generally physically able to do the things you want to do? ☐

Do you believe that you look after your body? ☐

Does your health limit your activities? ☐

Are you well-coordinated? ☐

Do you like what you see in the mirror? ☐

Do you go to the gym? ☐

Do you play sports? ☐

Do you do outdoor activities such as climbing and mountain biking? ☐

Do you swim regularly? ☐

Do you do yoga, tai chi or pilates? ☐

Is your work physically demanding? ☐

Do you regularly see a physiotherapist or chiropractor? ☐

Use the space below to make notes about your relationship with your body

_____

_____

_____

_____

_____

_____

_____

This isn't about beating yourself up, so avoid remarks like, 'I should get to the gym more' or, 'I ought to give yoga a try'. Instead, try to understand how you feel about your body. Is it a well-oiled machine that responds to your wishes, or is it a clumsy mess that you try not to think about? Maybe you have issues around body image, unable to like what you think you see in the mirror, despite reassurance from other people.

A mindful approach to movement, exercise and body image starts, of course, with acceptance. You are as you are at this point in time, but change is always possible.

ACCEPTANCE OF BODY ISSUES

Do a body scan, with the focus on acceptance. (The body scan technique is repeated in Appendix 1 for easy reference.) Make notes in the space below on any particularly difficult issues that you identify and spend a little time working on acceptance:

_____

_____

_____

_____

_____

_____

Mindful movement can be done formally, as a meditation, or informally, incorporated into your everyday life. Formal mindful movement is done very slowly, and purely for the sake of the movement so that it becomes a form of meditation in its own right.

A simple way to explore mindful movement is to start with stretches, which you can use as part of your preparation for sitting meditation. In fact if you are finding the physical stillness of sitting meditation difficult then you can use the various mindful movement exercises in this chapter as a preparation, to ease yourself in to the mental side of meditation. Do persevere with sitting meditation as well though.

 *Exercise 67*

SIMPLE MINDFUL MOVEMENT

Sit quietly for a few moments and focus on your breathing. Bring your attention onto one of your hands. Close the fingers into a fist (keep it loose) and then gently open the fist and stretch the fingers as far as you are able, straightening them and moving them apart from one another. Take it very slowly and let yourself feel each small movement of your fingers, palm and wrist. Feel the point at which the stretch begins to become uncomfortable (but not painful), and hold it there for a few seconds before relaxing.

Make notes about how it felt to do this.

_____

_____

_____

_____

_____

_____

The point where discomfort starts is often called 'the edge' and you can learn a lot from experiencing it. Are you inclined to wince and move quickly back to a more comfortable position, or do you tend to power through, forcing yourself to accept pain? Somewhere between the two extremes is a point of balance, where you work with the limits set by your body without abusing it, but at the same time gradually extending those limits.

→ Stretches

You can carry out any sequence of stretches mindfully. If you don't already have a stretching routine, try some of the following:

SITTING STRETCHES

Sit upright on a firm chair for these stretches.

▶ Raise your arms above your head, then bend from the waist to one side, then the other.

▶ Lift your legs until your knees are straight, point your toes. You can also do this stretch one leg at a time.

▶ Raise your arms to shoulder height, then straighten them, twist from the waist first to one side and then to the other.

LYING STRETCHES

▶ Lying on your back, lift one leg as high as you can, hold it, lower it, then repeat with the other leg.

▶ Lying on your side, lift the upper leg as high as you can, hold it, lower it, then roll to the other side and repeat.

STANDING STRETCHES

▶ Raise your arms above your head, then bend from the waist to one side then the other.

▶ Lift one foot a little off the ground, point the toe. If your balance is poor you can hold on to something.

▶ Raise your arms to shoulder height, then straighten them, twist from the waist, first to one side and then to the other.

Exercise 68

MINDFUL STRETCHES

Choose one of the stretches from the list and carry it out mindfully –
very slowly, with mental focus, and feeling for the edge. Alternatively,
use a stretch that is part of your own fitness routine. Work gently with
your body and don't push it too hard.

Use the space below to make notes about the experience:

_____

_____

_____

_____

_____

_____

The very slow movements will bring you into quite a different
awareness of your body. You'll feel each little change as your muscles
work to obey the instructions your mind is sending.

→ Formal mindful walking

All formal mindful movement is done very slowly, but it is mindful
walking that creates a form of meditation. It is just as intense and
focussed as sitting meditation. It can seem very strange at first, but stick
with it, like all new ideas it needs time.

You'll need a private place where you can take just a few steps in a
straight line. If you can be outdoors that brings the extra benefits of
fresh air, but you won't want to feel overlooked and self-conscious
while doing this exercise so it's more likely that you'll find an indoor
space, perhaps the room that you meditate in. Wear loose clothing
and if possible have bare feet. The key to formal mindful walking is
to do everything super-slowly, much more slowly than in the previous
exercises, and much more slowly than you think is possible.

Exercise 69

FORMAL MINDFUL WALKING

Stand still and straight, arms loosely by your sides, and allow your mind to settle and your body to be stable and balanced. Take your awareness to your contact with the ground or floor beneath your feet, then take your attention to your breathing and observe a few breaths. When you are ready, prepare to take the first step. Engage mentally with the idea of walking and focus your attention on one of your heels. Lift your heel slowly – very slowly – until it is off the ground. As your knee bends, lift your toes and slowly, slowly bring the foot forward. Slowly lower the foot to the floor, completing one step. Slowly, slowly repeat the process to take another step. Allow your mind to be fully engaged with the process of slow walking. Notice the many small movements that go to make up a step, and how your body anticipates each one, and makes constant corrections and adjustments. At the end of your space, make a slow turn and slowly, slowly, walk back. Stand still for a few moments, feeling the rhythms in your body.

Use the space below to make notes about your experience:

_____

_____

_____

_____

_____

_____

→ Informal mindful walking

Informal mindful walking is more like just going for a walk but with certain conditions that turn it into a mindful experience.

▶ Walk somewhere familiar, where you know you will be safe and where you don't need to look at a map. A green space such as a park is ideal, but if this isn't possible choose somewhere quiet and peaceful.

▶ Walk where you won't need to cross roads or worry about traffic.

▶ Make your first walk no longer than half an hour.

▶ Either carry nothing, or use a rucksack so that your arms are free and you are well-balanced.

▶ Turn off your phone.

▶ It's easier to do this on your own, since you will need to be silent.

▶ You can walk with or without an ultimate destination, but don't set a time for arrival.

 **Exercise 70**

INFORMAL MINDFUL WALKING

Choose a time and place for your walk and set off. Focus your awareness on your breathing at first, and allow your mind to clear of thoughts. Once you have settled into a comfortable walking rhythm, allow your awareness to move through your body, rather like a walking body scan. Then move your awareness out into the environment you are in, feel the air on your face, hear the sounds around you, smell the smells.

Use the space below to make notes about the experience:

_____

_____

_____

_____

_____

_____

This is another exercise that you can use if you are finding it difficult to adapt to sitting meditation. However, even though you may feel more comfortable with the familiar act of walking, it can actually be even more difficult to let go of thoughts during a mindful walk than it is during sitting meditation. Many of us use a walk as think-time and it's easy to slip into autopilot while you are walking. Of course this can be a useful tool for problem solving and organizing your thoughts, but during a mindful walk, make a conscious decision not to engage with your thoughts.

→ Mindful movement in everyday life

Once you have practised formal and informal mindful movement you can bring your new body-awareness into your everyday life. Many tasks can be carried out with informal mindful movement, without compromising safety or performance but with focus on the movements involved rather than allowing your mind to race away on its own. In other words, mindful movement is a way of coming out of autopilot, although you engage with the movements rather than the task. For this reason mundane tasks such as washing up, peeling potatoes, cleaning a car or mowing grass all provide opportunities for informal mindful movement.

Exercise 71

EVERYDAY MINDFUL MOVEMENT

Look at the list you made at the beginning of Chapter 1 and decide which items could incorporate mindful movement. In the examples given, you could choose 'going to the gym' or 'going for a run', whereas it wouldn't be sensible to choose 'putting the children to bed' when clearly your mindful focus should be on your interactions with your children. Choose a task to carry out with mindful movement – if there is nothing on your list that seems appropriate then choose a new task. Proceed at normal speed (although you might find you are a little slower than normal) and switch off distractions such as your radio or MP3.

Use the space below to make notes about the experience:

_____

_____

_____

_____

_____

_____

Making the choice to move mindfully is like giving yourself a three-minute breathing space while you are on the move. If you're having a really stressful and busy time you can incorporate informal mindful movement into your day, giving yourself a short mental break from everything that is crowding in on you. For instance, if you have a short walk at lunchtime, to the canteen or sandwich shop, you can choose to do this mindfully rather than making a phone call or sending a text while you walk. Similarly walking from a station or car park to your place of work can be done mindfully.

 Exercise 72

INCORPORATING MINDFUL MOVEMENT

Look at ways you can incorporate mindful walking into your normal routine. You can use the various lists you've already made, or start from scratch.

_____

_____

_____

_____

_____

_____

→ Mindful movement and fitness activities

 Exercise 73

YOUR FITNESS WORK

Make a list of any activities you do that contribute to your fitness. As well as sports and training, include activities such as dancing and cycling. Even gardening and housework can be included if they are vigorous enough.

Once you have done this, add a wish list of anything that you would like to do but don't do at the moment. If you don't do anything at all for fitness then your entire list will be things that you would like to do.

_____

_____

_____

_____

_____

_____

_____

_____

A lot of fitness training is repetitive, and so too are other activities. Both sorts lend themselves to informal mindful movement. On the other hand, actually playing sport may not be so adaptable. During a match or race you need to be mentally engaged with the activity, your opponents, your tactics and so on rather than with your actual physical movements.

Exercise 74

CHOOSING ACTIVITIES

Look through your list and decide which activities lend themselves to mindful movement. Do the same for your wish list, and also ask yourself why you don't currently do these activities. You may see one or more that only require you to find the motivation.

Having chosen your activity, carry it out mindfully. Turn off your MP3, clear your mind, and focus on your movements. Use the space below to make notes about the experience:

_____

_____

_____

_____

_____

_____

→ Benefits of mindful movement

STRETCHING

Simple stretching is known to have considerable health benefits for flexibility, co-ordination, posture and pain relief. Done mindfully it will also help with stress and tension and improve your sense of well-being.

BEING

Mindful movement is a way of Being in the moment.

YOUR BODY

Greater awareness of your body will make you more sensitive to its needs, and your mind and body will become more integrated.

YOUR MIND

Regular mindful movement, especially informal walking, will help you calm and settle your mind.

MOOD ENHANCER

Walking at normal speeds for more than 20 minutes at a time can help lift your mood as research shows this changes your brain chemistry. If you also walk mindfully you will add to this basic benefit.

IMPROVED AWARENESS AND BALANCE

The wobbliness that you may feel while walking very slowly is due to you becoming more aware of how your body constantly adjusts to keep you balanced. The more you practise this, the more balanced you will become.

→ Dealing with difficulties

MENTAL DISTRACTION

By now you know that in all mindfulness exercises you are vulnerable to mental distraction – your mind wanders, or chaotic thoughts overwhelm you. If you feel you can't stop thinking, remember to stand back and observe the thoughts rather than engage with them. Don't feel you've failed because they are there, just notice them and let them float through your mind. Similarly, if you suddenly realize you've been deep in thought instead of mindfully focussed on breathing and movement, there's no need to beat yourself up about it. Just gently bring your attention back to where it needs to be and carry on with the exercise.

BALANCE

If you find it really hard to balance during formal mindful walking, then try fixing your eyes on a point a little ahead, and keep looking at it as you walk. If you still feel unsteady, then walk next to a wall or fence and use that to steady you.

Developing your skills

▶ Revisit the questions in Exercise 65 and monitor changes in your attitude to your body.

▶ Continue to explore formal mindful walking.

▶ Every day do one task with mindful movement – choose tasks that you can do alone and quietly.

▶ Use your experience of exploring the edge of physical discomfort to help you with emotional discomfort. You can learn to stay with and accept both.

▶ Try a short formal walking meditation followed by a sitting meditation – this will help you extend the time of your sessions.

▶ Look for a location where you can safely walk aimlessly (a park or open space for instance). Experience walking and meditating with no destination in mind.

▶ Use mindful movement in fitness work and during other repetitive activities.

What have I learnt?

→ What have you learnt about your relationship with your body?

_____

_____

_____

_____

_____

➜ What have you learnt about informal mindful movement?

_____

_____

_____

_____

_____

➜ What have you learnt about formal mindful movement?

_____

_____

_____

_____

_____

➜ What have you learnt about mindfulness and fitness?

_____

_____

_____

_____

_____

Where to next?

While body scans teach you to make contact with your body, and experience it while in a static state of rest, mindful movement is more dynamic. This chapter has taken you into another aspect of your physicality, engaging with all the movements, big and small, that your body makes. Accepting your body as it is now often presents a challenge but through mindfully engaging with it you can appreciate what it does for you rather than its perceived shortcomings.

In the next chapter you will start from a position of accepting everything about yourself and move on to generating positive feelings about yourself, other people and the world around you. This too can be quite a challenge but everything you have read so far and all the exercises have prepared you for it.

10 smiling and loving-kindness

In this chapter you will learn:

In this chapter you will learn:
▶ about loving yourself
▶ about loving other people
▶ about giving.

Loving-kindness is a powerful meditation that takes mindfulness to a whole new level. For many people it is the ultimate life-changing meditation, and while this isn't the case for everyone there are still great benefits to be had from it. There is no rush to try it, in fact it's best to spend time exploring mindfulness and breathing meditation first. Once you have established a routine for meditation, have dealt with any difficulties and have begun to absorb mindfulness into your life, you can then turn your attention to loving-kindness.

Exercise 75

FINDING THE BEST IN PEOPLE

This exercise is about looking for the good things in people. You can choose anything that occurs to you – personality traits such as 'caring' or 'hardworking', actions such as 'keeps the office tidy', or 'created a beautiful garden' or behaviours such as 'never forgets a birthday' or 'kind to an elderly neighbour'. Write down whatever occurs to you that is positive.

Think of someone you are close to, and write down three good things about them:

1 _____

_____

_____

_____

_____

_____

2 _____

_____

_____

_____

_____

_____

3 _____

_____

_____

_____

_____

_____

Think of someone you are friendly with, and write down three good things about them:

1 _____

_____

_____

_____

_____

_____

2 _____

_____

_____

_____

_____

_____

3 _____

_____

_____

_____

_____

_____

Write down three kind or positive acts by complete strangers:

1 _____

_____

_____

_____

_____

2 _____

_____

_____

_____

_____

3 _____

_____

_____

_____

_____

Think of someone you rather dislike, and write down three good things about them:

1 _____

_____

_____

_____

_____

_____

2 _____

_____

_____

_____

_____

_____

3 _____

_____

_____

_____

_____

_____

Finally, write down three good things about yourself:

1 _____

_____

_____

_____

_____

_____

2 _____

_____

_____

_____

_____

_____

3 _____

_____

_____

_____

_____

_____

How was that? Did you find it steadily more difficult as you worked through the stages of the exercise? It's not surprising that we lose sight of the good qualities in people we dislike, but it is surprising how tough it can be to recognize our own good qualities. This is not the case for everyone of course, but whichever part of the exercise you found difficult gives you an insight into an aspect of yourself.

Exercise 76

FACING DIFFICULTIES

Write down what you found difficult about Exercise 75, and why you think this might be. For instance you may have been criticized heavily as a child, and find it difficult to escape from that criticism. Or you may have such an intense dislike of someone that you can't see any good in them at all.

_____

_____

_____

_____

_____

_____

Whatever your issues are, you can acknowledge them, start to accept them, and begin the process of letting go. Next though you're going to consider your more positive responses.

Look back at Exercise 75 and choose something that produced a positive response in you as you thought about it – a warm glow, or a smile. For instance, thinking about someone you are fond of might produce this response, or remembering an act of kindness by a stranger. Whatever you choose, you are going to focus on that person and that quality for the next exercise.

Choose somewhere private for Exercises 77, 78 and 79 as you need to feel quite unselfconscious.

SMILING

Make yourself comfortable and give yourself a few moments to settle, focussing on your breathing and letting your mind clear. Then bring to mind the person you have chosen to think about and their good qualities. Enjoy the positive feelings that produces. Allow yourself to smile, allow the smile to start in your eyes and spread gently into your face and the rest of your body. Let every piece of you feel the smile.

Use the space below to make notes about your experience:

_____

_____

_____

_____

_____

_____

While it may feel strange at first, this type of gentle inward smiling produces feelings of relaxation and well-being and is often used by Buddhists (you may see it referred to as 'thalamus smile' or 'organic smile'). As you smile, you can let go of any negative thoughts and feelings.

→ Smiling meditations

It's easy, or it should be, to smile when thinking about something positive. Taking this a step further, you can deliberately encourage yourself to smile while being mindful. Even if you have good reason to be in a negative mood, you can still smile.

 *Exercise 78*

 ## SMILING BODY SCAN

Make yourself comfortable and conduct a full body scan. Pay your normal level of attention to every piece of your body, in the usual order (see Chapter 7, Exercise 57, if you need to remind yourself of how to do this). This time add smiling to your body scan. As you focus on each part of your body imagine yourself directing a smile towards it and allowing yourself to appreciate that particular part of your body and what it does for you.

Use the space below to make notes about your experience:

_____

_____

_____

_____

_____

_____

Body scan is a mindfulness exercise with very specific procedure, but you can also add smiling to a walking meditation. This time the smile is not directed towards any particular part of you.

Exercise 79

SMILING AND WALKING

Choose to do a walking meditation and add a gentle, soft smile as you focus on your breathing. This smile is entirely for you, so enjoy it. Use the following space to make notes about your experience:

_____

_____

_____

_____

_____

You can also add smiling to three-minute breathing spaces, sitting meditation and everyday mindfulness. Experiment and find out what works best for you. Use the following space to keep records:

Smiling three-minute breathing space:

_____

_____

_____

_____

_____

Smiling sitting meditation:

_____

_____

_____

_____

_____

Smiling every day mindfulness:

_____

_____

_____

_____

_____

→ Benefits of smiling meditation

HEALTH

Research has been shown that smiling (and laughing) have a positive effect on mental and physical health. Smiling changes brain chemistry for the better in ways that researchers are still investigating.

MOOD

If you are feeling sad or depressed, and don't feel like smiling, doing it anyway will actually lift your mood. It's thought that just using your smile muscles signals to your brain that you are feeling happier.

STRESS

Smiling has been shown to create calmness and reduce stress.

RELATIONSHIPS

Smiling is like yawning – it's catching, and people respond positively to a smile.

→ Loving-kindness

Loving-kindness is a very specific meditation that builds on the idea of extending kindly feelings to everything and everybody.

There is no special posture for loving-kindness meditation. You can sit, lie or even walk, but aim to be as physically comfortable and as stable as possible. To start with however, it's best to sit in your usual meditation posture, so that you can use the familiarity you have already established. You'll see that this meditation includes elements of visualization, which is brought in after a few moments of clearing your mind and letting go of any emotions.

Ultimately the meditation will take you to a place where you can find positive feelings for everything – not just people but everything in the universe. Clearly this is a big ambition, but the journey starts in a familiar place, with your relationship with yourself. This is the one relationship that will always be there, the longest and deepest you will ever have. If you can't love yourself, then all loving is likely to prove difficult.

During loving-kindness meditation you'll think about yourself in a positive way and then take your mind to your wishes for yourself. Look as deep as you can. You may be currently wishing for anything from a new gadget to a solution to a particular problem, but behind those wishes are your deeper desires. Allow your mind to form the actual words as wishes for yourself. For example:

 May I be calm. May I be free of hatred. May I be loving.

You will find your own wishes, and your wishes will change with each meditation.

 ## Exercise 80

 ## WISHES FOR YOURSELF

Think about your current wishes for yourself and write them down. Start with the obvious ones that we all have such as, 'I wish I wasn't so busy' or, 'I wish I was thinner'. Write them down to clear them out of your mind, but then take a little longer to explore your deeper wishes for yourself:

_____

_____

_____

_____

_____

_____

Now you can take these deeper wishes for yourself into a meditation. If it helps, you can visualize yourself as a small child, and imagine the wishes you would have for that child.

Exercise 81

LOVING-KINDNESS FOR YOURSELF

Make yourself comfortable, and take a few moments to relax. Focus on your breathing and use your awareness of your breathing to take you fully into your body. Let your mind clear of thoughts and feelings. After a few minutes start to think about yourself in a kindly way, recalling the positive qualities you've already identified. When you are ready, explore your wishes for yourself and allow the words to form in your mind.

Use the space below to make notes about your experience:

_____

_____

_____

_____

_____

_____

If you found this difficult, repeat it a few times. Don't hurry on to the next stages of loving-kindness, which move your attention to wishing well towards other people. Explore what it means to want good things for yourself, and take time to discover which things are the most important to you. If you feel unworthy of this attention, then it's important to repeat the meditation until you grow more comfortable with the idea that you deserve to be loved.

Keep records of how you progress in this, and note any changes that occur in your relationship with yourself.

Use the space below to make notes:

_____

_____

_____

_____

_____

· ·

When you feel ready, expand your loving-kindness meditations outwards. You can do the following exercise in one go, or by building gradually, adding a stage at each session.

LOVING-KINDNESS

Always start with a loving-kindness meditation focussed on yourself. After a while, move your attention away from yourself towards other people. At each stage, stay with it long enough for the feelings of loving-kindness to appear. Once you experience the feeling, dwell on it for a while.

▶ Start with someone you respect and look up to. Bring them to mind, visualize them in detail, then wish them well – let the words form in your mind.

▶ Move on to someone you care about in a personal way – a friend or family member. Bring them to mind also, then wish them well. Let the words form in your mind.

▶ Then think about someone you know but have neutral feelings about, and wish them well in the same way.

▶ Now consider someone you don't get on well with at the moment. When you bring them to mind, allow time for any negative thoughts to weaken, then take the time to wish them well in your heart.

▶ Bring all four people into your mind together – yourself, someone you care about, someone you have neutral feelings about and someone you don't get on with. Practise extending your loving-kindness to the whole group.

▶ Allow your feelings to move outwards from the group to encompass everyone you know and people you don't know. Let the feeling grow to include all animals, all life, and finally, the entire universe. You could start by thinking of an entire community that you already know, and moving outwards from there to other communities and so on.

Initially loving-kindness is practised like a formal sitting meditation, but once you get a feel for it you can take it out into the world. In your everyday life you can face the world with a friendly, open attitude, assuming the best about everyone you meet. This will be less intense than a solitary meditation session, but loving-kindness can be practised at any level.

 *Exercise 83*

EVERYDAY LIFE

When you have tried loving-kindness meditations a few times and started to make progress, look at ways you can take it out into the world. Start with something in which you already expect positive responses, such as a meeting with friends, before moving on to more challenging situations.

Use the space below to make notes.

_____

_____

_____

_____

_____

_____

→ Loving and giving

It's only a small step from loving to giving. When you wish for good things for someone, you are giving them that wish, even though they don't know it. Think of giving in its broadest sense, not just presents, or giving something to charity. You can give someone a smile, or a kind word, or a helping hand for instance. You can give your time and your attention. These are all mindful ways of giving, in which you are fully present in the act of giving. If you try to do one act of mindful kindness every day, however small, you will feel better for it.

 **Exercise 84**

GIVING

Ask yourself 'what have I given today?' Include even the smallest gifts, such as a smile to a stranger or letting someone rushed take your place in a queue.

Use the space below to make notes:

_____

_____

_____

_____

_____

_____

_____

_____

→ Benefits of loving-kindness

SELF

The more you come to accept that you are as worthy of kindness as anyone else, the more you will feel peaceful, calm and comfortable in your own skin.

SELFLESSNESS

Repeating this meditation will help you feel disinterested generosity towards everyone. Your interactions with the people you've tended to dislike will change for the better, and almost certainly they will respond in positive ways, improving your relationship with them.

POSITIVITY

Prejudices and negative attitudes will fall away as you repeat the meditation, and you will be happier as a result. You'll be able to let go of any negative mental habits that you have. You'll be happy when other people do well, rather than feeling jealous.

OPTIMISM

Looking for the best in people and in life generally will help you be more optimistic and optimistic people are generally happier than pessimists. The world won't have changed, just your attitude to it.

FLEXIBILITY

We all have prejudices, and over time they can become set in stone. Loving-kindness helps us confront and challenge them and the process of doing that opens the mind and makes it more flexible and receptive to new ideas.

HAPPINESS

It's hard to be happy if you are full of jealousies and insecurities, if you are yearning for more possessions or mired down in self-criticism. Loving-kindness teaches you to like yourself, and to be happy for the good things that happen to other people.

COMPASSION AND EMPATHY

Loving-kindness creates a more caring and compassionate approach, developing your ability to both empathize with other people's difficulties and relish their good fortune. Even when you dislike someone, you'll start to have compassion for them.

→ Dealing with difficulties

FEELING NOTHING

There is no need to force yourself. Try bringing different people to mind, or wait for another day. Have regular short loving-kindness sessions and move gently towards your kindly feelings. They will grow in time.

FEELING TOO MUCH

If you find the meditation brings up strong feelings, then take it gently. Have short sessions, and build slowly towards the complete meditation. Detachment is still important, in the sense that you aim to feel about others in a kindly but disinterested way.

PITY

It's easy for empathy to turn into pity, and pity often includes an element of superiority. Accept that this has happened, and allow it to fade away.

LUST

Sexual feelings aren't appropriate during this meditation and will only serve to distract you, so avoid bringing to mind anyone who arouses those feelings in you. Wish those people well as part of the wider group towards the end of the meditation.

VULNERABILITY

Taking loving-kindness out into the world can feel quite scary, but having an open, warm attitude doesn't mean that you have to let go of caring for your personal safety, or of protecting your cash, cards or PIN. Allow these essential protective behaviours to become second nature and run them in the background.

Developing your skills

▶ Revisit the questions in Exercise 75 and continue to work on finding good things in a whole range of people.

▶ Repeat the smiling meditation frequently.

▶ Gradually take organic smiling into your daily life – start by finding a reason to smile at least once a day.

▶ Explore loving-kindness at your own pace.

What have I learnt?

→ What have you learnt about extending loving-kindness towards yourself?

_____

_____

_____

_____

_____

→ What have you learnt about extending loving-kindness to others?

_____

_____

_____

_____

_____

➜ What have you learnt about giving?

_____

_____

_____

_____

_____

Where to next?

Loving-kindness represents a huge step in your progress towards mindfulness. Some people would say it is the final step, but there is always more to learn. It is an ongoing process. You won't develop all your practice at all times – sometimes you'll want to focus on sitting meditation, which is the bedrock of all mindfulness, and at other times you'll be developing other aspects, perhaps looking at your own needs, or your relationship with your body. Loving-kindness is part of this overall picture and now that you have experienced it you'll return to it in your own time, when you are ready.

Mindfulness is not a programme with a beginning, middle and end. It is an attitude, an approach to life. In the next chapter you'll learn something about how mindfulness can help you deal with that bane of modern life, stress.

11

Mindfulness and stress

In this chapter you will learn:
▶ about different types of stress
▶ how to assess your stress levels
▶ about the mindful approach to stress.

Stress and stress-related illnesses have had a lot of publicity in recent years and yet many of us continue with ways of living that only increase our stress, or rather, increase our bad stress. It's often forgotten that there is such a thing as good stress, which means just enough stimulus in life to keep a person interested, focussed and motivated. Bad stress starts when we take on too much and feel overwhelmed and out of control.

Life events such as divorce, bereavement, illness, and money worries can be unavoidably stressful, especially if they happen close together. In addition, a lifestyle with no down time built into it produces ongoing long-term stress.

Exercise 85

LOOK AT YOUR STRESS

Make a list of stressful events that have happened to you over the last 18 to 24 months. As well as obviously negative events, consider any event that involved substantial changes, such as a house move or retirement.

_____

_____

_____

_____

_____

_____

_____

_____

_____

The more challenging events you have listed, the more likely you are to be stressed. However while big life-changing events are always stressful, they don't necessarily produce unacceptable levels of stress in an individual. It will depend on your core nature, on what you have learnt from your life experiences, and on the condition you are in at that particular moment in your life.

Stress can also come from the ways in which you live your life. If you have a demanding job, take on too much, are always running late, tend to worry about things, don't eat well and don't get enough exercise then you will probably be stressed. If you're unemployed, worried about losing your job, worried about health matters or in poor housing you are equally likely to be stressed.

LIFESTYLE STRESS

Look at lifestyle factors that may be adding to your stress. Consider your family life, work life, relationships, finances, housing, health and anything else that you find stressful. Make a note of them below:

_____

_____

_____

_____

_____

_____

_____

Now you're starting to form a picture of how stressed you are and why. Stress quickly becomes a vicious circle, so that you find yourself behaving in ways that only add to your stress.

Exercise 87

MONITORING YOUR BEHAVIOURS

Tick the box for each of the following that you answer yes to.

Do you regularly eat snacks and junk food? ☐

Do you regularly rush meals or eat on the go? ☐

Are you too busy to make time to relax? ☐

Do you have to have things done your way? ☐

Do you feel you have to do everything? ☐

Are you irritable? ☐

Are you impatient if there is a delay? ☐

Do you take on too much? ☐

Is your life chaotic? ☐

Do you take things too seriously? ☐

Do you forget to ask for help? ☐

Do you keep putting things off? ☐

Are you too busy for holidays? ☐

Do you feel overwhelmed? ☐

Do you feel guilty if you take a break? ☐

Are you too busy to take exercise? ☐

Do you feel breathless, shaky or sweaty? ☐

Do you find it difficult to talk things through? ☐

Do you feel hard done by? ☐

Do you ignore your stress? ☐

Does it all seem pointless at times? ☐

Do you feel isolated? ☐

These questions are all about behaviours that are the result of stress but also, for the most part, add to it. We all do some of them some of the time, but if you answered Yes to eight or more questions, then you are showing signs of stress – and the more Yes answers, the more stress.

At this point you may be wondering, why does it matter? Basically stress is physically and mentally bad for people – the key to this is in the ongoing nature of modern-day stressors. Human beings seem to have evolved to live simple subsistence lives as hunter-gatherers and later as farmers. This evolution included a response to danger, known as the fight-or-flight mechanism, which cuts in when there is a threat, providing the physical energy to either run away or fight back.

As soon as the danger is over, your body returns, or should return, to normal. The trouble starts when stress is ongoing and long-term, because the fight-or-flight mechanism can become permanently switched on and it becomes the new normal. The body is constantly flooded with adrenalin and other chemicals and over enough time this has a negative effect both physically and mentally.

Being constantly on the alert, wound-up or wired is uncomfortable enough to cause us to look for relief. But rather than deal with the source of the stress we often respond in unhealthy ways, adding to the damage.

RESPONSES TO STRESS

Answer 'Never', 'Sometimes' or 'Always' to the following questions:

Do you comfort eat?	Never/Sometimes/Always
Do you forget to eat?	Never/Sometimes/Always
Do you need alcohol to relax?	Never/Sometimes/Always
Do you use recreational drugs to relax?	Never/Sometimes/Always
Does spending money make you feel better?	Never/Sometimes/Always
Do you get through on caffeine?	Never/Sometimes/Always
Are you too busy for friends and family?	Never/Sometimes/Always

Do you take regular short breaks?	Never/Sometimes/Always
Do you get regular exercise?	Never/Sometimes/Always
Do you keep up your social life?	Never/Sometimes/Always
Do you pursue leisure activities?	Never/Sometimes/Always
Do you meditate?	Never/Sometimes/Always

The more 'Always' answers you have to the first seven questions, the more likely it is that your response to stress is damaging you in some way. Your 'Sometimes' answers may be flagging up a warning. The last five questions are about healthier ways to manage stress, so the more 'Always' answers the better.

Looking at the healthy ways of managing stress you can see that they often consist of a break, a change of focus and in some cases contact with other people. Meditation and mindfulness offer you additional healthy ways of approaching stress that have added benefits. They will help you achieve insight, and perhaps that will lead to you making changes that reduce your stress levels.

All of the healthy ways of managing stress have one thing in common – they involve doing something for yourself. At difficult times in your life it can feel as if you are the least important person and that there is just no time for your own needs.

Let's return to the earlier example of the woman in the supermarket whose children have run amok. Perhaps if we knew the whole story we would see that she was stressed and failing to take care of herself properly. Perhaps her father is ill and her partner is worried about losing his job. She is tired and needs a break, but she says to herself, 'At least I've got my health, and it's crucial now that I hang on to my job, I must just keep going'. She is talking herself out of caring for herself because it feels selfish and unimportant, and yet what's the result? She gets more and more tired, more and more unhappy, and in a worst case scenario her health breaks down, either physically or mentally, and she's of no use to her father, her partner or her children.

In other words, when stress strikes, it's time to start taking care of yourself. The next exercise is sometimes quite emotional so allow plenty of time to sit quietly after the meditation is finished.

Exercise 89

LOVING-KINDNESS OF SELF

Carry out a loving-kindness meditation focussed entirely on yourself and explore in detail all your good wishes for yourself. You may find if difficult, but persevere. However you're feeling about yourself right at this moment, wish yourself only good things. Form the words firmly in your mind. Imagine yourself as a child and give yourself a comforting hug.

Seeing yourself as a child, vulnerable and perhaps unhappy, is what sometimes releases a well of emotions. If this happens to you, allow the emotions to run their course while you wait quietly, caring but detached.

Use the space below to make notes:

_____

_____

_____

_____

_____

_____

The fight-or-flight mechanism is designed for action and so it ensures that stress affects us physically, providing the instant energy that your muscles need. If, for instance, you are running late for an appointment, and stuck in traffic, you can neither fight nor flee, and yet your body will start to prepare for you to do one or the other.

When you are unable to take physical action, as is so often the case, then the chemicals generated by the fight-or-flight mechanism stay in your body, causing a range of uncomfortable sensations.

Physical symptoms of stress

Remember: do not use this list as a diagnostic tool – see your doctor if necessary.

- ▶ Flushing
- ▶ Tense muscles
- ▶ Fidgeting
- ▶ Sweating
- ▶ Acid indigestion
- ▶ Heart pounding

- ▶ Shallow rapid breathing
- ▶ Dry mouth
- ▶ Feeling you can't swallow
- ▶ Nausea
- ▶ Needing the loo

Exercise 90

WHERE DO YOU FEEL YOUR STRESS?

Look at the list of physical stress symptoms and assess where in your body you feel stress. Add anything extra that occurs to you – everyone is different. If you find this difficult, use a visualization of a stressful event to help you recall how stress feels to you.

Use the space below to make notes:

_____

_____

_____

_____

_____

_____

_____

→ Mindful ways of managing stress

Now that you have pinpointed your vulnerable areas, you can use a body scan to target them. As you breathe into that part of you, imagine the breath soothing and relaxing you, and as you breathe out, imagine the stress leaving your body.

If you do this regularly you will release any ongoing physical stress, creating a background of lower stress in your life. The benefits can be immediate but the most lasting effects are cumulative, so don't use body scan as a quick fix.

You can, however, choose to use the three-minute breathing space in this way. If the day is proving difficult and you can feel the tensions building up, then find a way to take a little time out for a breathing space. You can apply this to many stressful situations. As long as you have practised and become familiar with the breathing space exercise, and you take account of safety issues, you can gain some immediate benefit from even a few seconds of mindfulness.

Your biggest support during the process of change though will be your regular daily meditation. There is something almost magical in the way that by clearing your mind and letting go of all thoughts changes begin to happen without your active involvement. It's almost as if your mind was ready to get on with it, but just needed you to stand back and stop interfering with the process.

→ Making changes

If you think about it, stress comes from two sources:

▶ external factors, such as a job loss or bereavement
▶ internal factors, where the choices you make lead you to being overstretched and stressed.

EXTERNAL FACTORS

There is not much you can do about the actual events – they happen to you, but you are not in control of them. This is true even if the event is a problem with your own health and even if your lifestyle has contributed to your health problem. Whatever the events are, it's easy to feel that you are a victim of circumstances, with no control over your own life. In most situations the only thing you can change is yourself, and mindful detachment will help you see that this is true of even the biggest stressful event. You may need to start with acknowledgement and acceptance, since it is easy to go into denial when confronted with something deeply distressing.

Exercise 91

ACKNOWLEDGE AND ACCEPT

The list you made in Exercise 85 is all about external events that have caused you stress. How far do you resist accepting that these things have happened, and are you putting energy into resistance and denial? Is the list complete or are there events that you refuse to acknowledge as stressful? Go back to the list and fine-tune it.

INTERNAL FACTORS

Sometimes your stress is largely of your own making, although it's unlikely to feel like that. However, the choices you make in life can produce stress if they are driven by deep-rooted beliefs about yourself and the world that are not helpful. Here are some examples of beliefs and attitudes that can lead to stress:

▶ I need to rush as there's so much to do.

▶ I have to aim high.

▶ I have to be successful.

▶ The world's against me.

▶ I have to fight for what I want.

▶ I mustn't say 'No'.

▶ I never get appreciation.

▶ I never get respect.

▶ I'm always overworked.

▶ I'm the responsible one.

▶ I'm alone with my problems.

▶ People are so annoying.

 *Exercise 92*

CHECKING YOUR BELIEFS AND ATTITUDES

Look through the list of internal factors and select any items that you recognize in yourself. Write them out below, and add anything else that you think of.

_____

_____

_____

_____

_____

_____

_____

_____

_____

_____

You may need to repeat this exercise over time, as your self-knowledge grows and matures.

Now that you've acknowledged how your behaviours, beliefs and attitudes are contributing to your stress, you can look at ways of making changes.

→ Making changes: behaviour

Whether your stress comes from external factors, or internal, or both, you can look at ways of changing your responses which will reduce the level of your stress. First of course you need to know what the changes are going to be. Look at your answers to the first seven questions in Exercise 88 and focus on your 'Always' answers for the next exercise, adding in any 'Sometimes' answers where it seems appropriate, and any other behaviours that you recognize in yourself.

For both kinds of stress you can choose to make changes to your responses. Repeating the loving-kindness meditation will help you prepare for the changes, and your regular daily breathing meditation will create the calm mental space where you can implement those changes.

Exercise 93

RESPONSES

Go back to the answers in Exercise 88 and use them to create a list of responses where you can see it would help you to make changes. Leave Column B empty for now.

COLUMN A   COLUMN B

_____   _____

_____   _____

_____   _____

_____   _____

_____   _____

_____   _____

_____   _____

_____   _____

_____   _____

_____   _____

_____   _____

· ·

Whether your list is long or short, don't try to change everything at once – **that** will only add to your stress. Start with whatever seems easiest to change, and decide how you will start to change that one item. As an example, look at the following list:

COLUMN A

Wine in the evening   _____

Comfort eating   _____

Too much caffeine   _____

No exercise   _____

This is a fairly typical list, but each of us would approach the changes differently, depending on what seemed the easiest to tackle first. So, in the next exercise you will tailor your list to your own preferences, choosing the order for tackling the changes.

You will also decide how you will make the changes. They key is to take it gently, in small steps. This is a good basic principle, and also with some things, such as giving up caffeine, you don't want to shock your system with a sudden cold turkey – you'll only end up with a withdrawal headache and feeling thoroughly miserable.

For example, the list above could be completed like this:

COLUMN A	COLUMN B
Wine in the evening	*first – no wine during the week*
Comfort eating	*fourth – stop buying ready meals and chocolate*
Too much caffeine	*third – cut down gradually, start at a weekend*
No exercise	*second – walk to station, join gym*

 Exercise 94

TAILORING THE LIST

Go back to Exercise 93 and in Column B indicate the order that you will tackle the items in, and how you will go about it.

While you are implementing the changes, be gentle with yourself. Don't set goals that are too tough – remember you are already stressed and don't want to add to the pressure. Use your mindfulness techniques to help you through any difficulties. For instance, someone who is trying to resist comfort eating might find themselves craving for chocolate. A little mindful detachment, standing back and observing the craving instead of engaging with it or having an internal dialogue about it, might be just enough to get them through a difficult moment.

→ Making changes: beliefs

If changing behaviours is tough, changing beliefs provides a whole extra level of difficulty. It is possible though, and like most things the more motivated you are the more you will achieve. You have begun to identify the beliefs and attitudes that could be feeding your stress and just that acknowledgement will help you along the path to change.

 *Exercise 95*

 BELIEFS

Return to the list you made in Exercise 92 and read it out loud. Use the space below to make notes about what you learnt by doing this.

_____

_____

_____

_____

_____

_____

_____

_____

_____

_____

_____

How did that feel? Sometimes just the act of saying something out loud gives you a new perspective on it. It can seem less true than it did inside your head, perhaps even a little silly or comical. Don't beat yourself up about this; you are on a journey of discovery and heading towards helpful change.

The next exercise may take some time, even if your list is a short one. Don't rush. Only address one item at a time so that you give it your full attention and you don't tire yourself mentally.

DECIDING TO CHANGE BELIEFS AND ATTITUDES

Take each item on your list and consider it in detail. For each one ask yourself:

How important is this to me really?

Do I cherish it?

Can I let go of it?

Allow yourself to feel kindly towards any difficulties it may have caused you, accept that you meant well, and wish for yourself the ability to change to a more helpful belief or attitude.

Changing beliefs and attitudes is an ongoing process. However, you can reduce much of your stress by taking a mindful approach, using body scans and breathing spaces and of course meditating daily.

Developing your skills

▶ Revisit the exercises and fine-tune your response.

▶ Consider any lifestyle changes you can make to help reduce your stress.

▶ As your self-awareness grows, you'll start to identify your unhelpful behaviours, beliefs and attitudes in real time, as they happen.

What have I learnt?

→ What have you learnt about the stress in your life?

_____

_____

_____

_____

_____

_____

_____

→ What have you learnt about your coping behaviours?

_____

_____

_____

_____

_____

_____

_____

→ What have you learnt about the changes that would be helpful to you?

_____

_____

_____

_____

_____

_____

_____

Where to next?

Stress often builds up over time without you realizing how bad it's becoming. By mindfully observing yourself and assessing your life events and your behaviours, you can begin to make the changes that will reduce your stress. A mindful attitude to life, with daily meditation, will give you a basis for staying calm at stressful times, and for making a quicker recovery after the stress has passed.

The last chapter in this Workbook looks at relationships and how mindfulness can help you improve all relationships and deepen your closest relationships.

12 Mindful relationships

In this chapter you will learn:
- ▶ to think about your relationships
- ▶ to acknowledge and accept
- ▶ to bring mindfulness to relationships.

When a mindful attitude is brought to relationships it can lead to beneficial changes. This is true of both your deeply emotional relationships (for instance with your parents, children or partner) and your more practical relationships (with neighbours, work colleagues or acquaintances). It is even true of the passing relationships you have in everyday life (shop workers, waiting staff, call centre operatives and so on).

Exercise 97

THINK ABOUT YOUR RELATIONSHIPS

Write a few words about your various types of relationship as they are at this moment in time. The following are some questions to help you get started, but if you have something else to say, then ignore the questions and say it. Ignore any that aren't relevant to your present situation. Try to give more than just a 'Yes' or 'No' answer.

Close relationships:

▶ If you're single, how happy are you with the way your romantic relationships progress? How would you like things to be different?

▶ If you have a partner, would you say the two of you were in a good place? What could be improved?

▶ Do you consider your immediate family to be supportive and nurturing? Do you enjoy their company?

▶ For you, what are the rewards and challenges of parenting?

_____

_____

_____

_____

_____

_____

_____

_____

Practical relationships:

▶ Is there a good atmosphere in your workplace?

▶ Do you generally get to know your neighbours?

▶ Are you active in your community?

▶ Do you find it easy to mix in a wide social group?

▶ Are you comfortable talking to authority figures such as a doctor or solicitor?

_____

_____

_____

_____

_____

_____

_____

Passing relationships:

▶ Do you find the service in shops generally good?
▶ Do you generally get what you need from help lines and call centres?
▶ Do you find yourself challenging bureaucracy?

_____

_____

_____

_____

_____

_____

_____

If you look at your notes you may be able to see a pattern emerging. You may, for instance, have a warm and supportive home life but find it difficult to mix in a wider social group. Or you may be confident when dealing with authority figures but shy in a romantic context.

Whether relationships are going well or badly, we tend to look to the other person for the reason, with thoughts like 'he's always so kind and helpful' or 'she always makes trouble'. Every relationship is actually a two-way street, so that if you see the helpful man in the distance you'll be smiling as you approach him, but the troublemaker will only ever see you looking defensive and ready for anything. In both cases your attitude will reinforce what is already going on between you. And of course your attitudes in general will have a profound impact on all your relationships.

Exercise 98

ASSESS YOUR ATTITUDES IN RELATIONSHIPS

For this exercise, divide your relationships into two groups. Use Column A for close relationships (family, partner, old friends and so on) and Column B for more distant relationships (work colleagues, neighbours, your doctor and dentist, and so on). For some you will have the same answers in both columns, and some questions will only seem relevant to one group or the other. Answer as you think fit in each case.

	A	B
	Close	**Distant**
Do you sulk if you lose an argument?	☐	☐
Do you understand your own feelings?	☐	☐
Do you find it easy to express yourself?	☐	☐
Do you bear a grudge?	☐	☐
Do you get anxious talking to authority figures?	☐	☐
Are you confident in expressing your feelings?	☐	☐

Can you see the other person's point of view?	☐	☐
Do you quickly go on the defensive?	☐	☐
Are you judgemental of others?	☐	☐
Do you take responsibility for your actions?	☐	☐
Do you have to be right?	☐	☐
Do you take criticism well?	☐	☐
Do you keep your thoughts to yourself?	☐	☐
Do you need to dominate conversations?	☐	☐
Are you thin-skinned?	☐	☐
Do you tend to keep quiet?	☐	☐
Do you dread meeting new people?	☐	☐
Do you enjoy closeness?	☐	☐
Do you blame others when things go wrong?	☐	☐
Do you worry about being dumped?	☐	☐
Are you needy?	☐	☐
Are you jealous?	☐	☐
Do you always have an agenda?	☐	☐
Are you easily lead?	☐	☐
Do you dislike giving presentations?	☐	☐
Is it best that no one knows the real you?	☐	☐

Many of the questions in this exercise relate to qualities most of us would prefer not to face up to. Having worked through this book though you've had some practice in being honest with yourself. Remember no one has to see your answers, so, if you need to, go back and redo the exercise. You've also had practice in being kind to yourself, so don't feel that acknowledging your negative qualities means that you have to beat yourself up about them.

You are you, and you can only start from where you're at, but as you now know change is always possible. And if you think about it, in the whole complicated process of building and running relationships the only aspect that is within your power to change is yourself.

You already know that the first steps towards change are acknowledgement and acceptance, so just by completing the exercise, and being honest with yourself, you've begun the process. Whatever you've learnt about yourself can't be unlearnt, and now that you're aware of your own habits you'll start to bring a mindful attitude to bear on them.

BE KIND TO YOURSELF

Allow yourself a loving-kindness meditation focussed entirely on you. If you learnt anything painful as a result of Exercise 98, face it and forgive yourself. Try to avoid defensiveness, explanation or resolutions to change or improve. This is just about soothing any hurt you may be feeling.

Look at the notes you made about your relationships and choose one that isn't going too well at the moment. However don't at this stage choose one that is of supreme importance, or one that is in an extremely bad state. Someone you have to interact with regularly and who irritates you in some way, such as a work colleague, fellow committee member or neighbour, would be about right.

WHAT'S GOING ON FOR ME?

Think about the relationship, about what goes wrong, and think particularly about your own part in it. Ask yourself:

Why does this bother me so much?

Would it bother me if someone else did it?

Is it all about our history?

Does the person concerned remind me of someone from the past?

Do I always struggle with people of this type or people in this role?

What are my expectations of this person and this relationship?

_____

_____

_____

_____

_____

_____

_____

_____

_____

. . . .

→ Loving-kindness

It's easy to think kindly of the people you are close to, and the people who are kind to you, but understandably harder to extend generous thoughts to anyone you dislike, or who has treated you badly. If you've been practising loving-kindness meditations then you'll already have some insight into how it feels to create good wishes for different categories of people.

You can use loving-kindness to focus on a specific relationship that is in difficulty.

⏰ Exercise 101

LOVING-KINDNESS

Take the time for a loving-kindness meditation focussed on the relationship you've already identified in Exercise 100. Let go of defensiveness, justification and explanation. Remember to start by focussing on your breathing and allow your mind to clear. Then:

▶ **Create good wishes for yourself such as: 'May I stay calm, and let go of my negative feelings towards this person'.**

▶ **Create good wishes for the person such as: 'May they feel calm and happy'.**

▶ **Create good wishes for the relationship such as: 'May we find our way to a warmer and more positive connection'.**

One effect of regular meditation is often described as opening up a space in your mind where you can consider responses instead of reacting on autopilot. As you continue with your daily meditation sessions you may well find that you become more self-aware and are able to start the process of change.

You can expect this to take time, as longstanding behaviours are always difficult to address, and often come from deep-rooted causes. In the short-term though you can learn to be a better listener, and see almost immediate changes in the way people relate to you, followed by changes in your response to them.

→ Mindful listening

You have already had a small taste of mindful listening when you did Exercise 5 in Chapter 1, which involved coming out of autopilot to interact fully with another person. In Exercise 40 in Chapter 5 you practised being patient, another important aspect of mindful listening. By all means repeat these exercises before moving on if you feel the need to.

Mindful listening helps in two important ways:

▶ In order to listen mindfully, you will have to put aside your judgements, preconceptions and any negative expectations of the person you are listening to. Perhaps as a result they will see you in a new light.

▶ By giving your full attention to what they are saying, you will hear them more clearly. Perhaps as a result you will see them in a new light.

There are various stages to mindful listening, and the first one is to understand yourself, your needs and any agenda you might have.

For example, you might always struggle to get on with a work colleague who doesn't seem to you to be pulling their weight, and yet no one else seems to mind. This could be part of a longstanding resentment that goes back to your childhood, for instance if younger siblings were never asked to do chores, or it could be part of a more recent problem with tiredness and being overloaded at work. Perhaps you are the only one directly affected by your colleague's laziness, or perhaps their laziness doesn't affect you at all but you still resent it. In order to understand the relationship, you have to first understand yourself.

Exercise 100 is designed to help you start on the path towards understanding your own issues, and you can repeat it as often as you need to, focussing on a different relationship each time.

Mindful listening is all about giving your full attention to the speaker, without judging them or yourself, and letting go of all your preconceptions and expectations. In other words, having understood and accepted your own issues and agendas, you can let go of them and take your focus to the other person.

 Mindful listening: hints and tips
- ▶ Decide to give your full attention to listening.
- ▶ Stop anything else you are doing.
- ▶ Clear your mind of your own issues and agendas.
- ▶ Listen to the person and hear what they are saying.
- ▶ Be aware of their body language.
- ▶ Be aware of their tone of voice and speed of speech.
- ▶ If thoughts come to you while listening, let them go.
- ▶ Let your responses encourage the talker.
- ▶ Don't try to change the subject.
- ▶ Try not to judge.

 *Exercise 102*

MINDFUL LISTENING

It's time to practise mindful listening. Ultimately you will use mindful listening to really hear the person who you identified in Exercise 100, but you may prefer to start with someone who you are on better terms with. It's up to you, but don't rush things. Also choose a time when you will do this, and be prepared for the conversation to take longer than normal.

Use the space below to make notes afterwards:

_____

_____

_____

_____

_____

_____

→ Putting it all together

The more you integrate mindfulness into your life, the easier it will be to bring mindful attitudes to your relationships. Daily meditation will help you be calmer and more detached, while breathing spaces are useful when things get difficult. Mindful listening is just a very specific way to live in the moment, giving your entire attention to the other person and what they are saying. In a broader sense, you can be fully with other people and fully engaged with them even if listening isn't part of that particular moment.

Acknowledgement and acceptance are also important in relationships. It's easy to waste energy longing for people to be different – you may want your partner to be romantic, or more glamorous, you may want your children to be high achievers, or to have inherited your talents and interests, you may wish your parents were less demanding or more up-to-date in their views. Whatever you want other people to be, it's unlikely to happen. Accepting them as they are is the first step towards improving your relationship.

Acceptance will be easier if you stand back from your own longings and fantasies – detachment will help you see the difference between unrealistic fantasies and reasonable desires. By being mindful you won't be settling for anything unsatisfactory or second rate, rather you will be achieving a healthy perspective, and making the best you can out of what you've got. You may even come to realize that it's time to accept that a relationship has changed irrevocably – it may be over, or moving into a new phase.

Exercise 103

ACKNOWLEDGEMENT, ACCEPTANCE AND DETACHMENT

Think about a relationship where there are currently difficulties and acknowledge what it is about the other person that disappoints, irritates or upsets you. Spend a little time accepting that this is how they are, and let go of your own frustrations.

Use the space below to make notes:

_____

_____

_____

_____

_____

_____

Relationships that aren't going well will always tend to demand the most attention, and be at the forefront of your thinking. Happy relationships can easily slip into the background, but they too need your attention, both to keep them on track and more simply so that you make sure you enjoy the happiness they bring you.

For the final exercise in this book you are going to choose a relationship that is going well and enjoy the moment.

Exercise 104

SOMEONE YOU LOVE

Consider all your different relationships and choose one that is full of love and happiness. Make a plan to spend some mindful time with that person. You can make this informal, the next time you happen to be together, or formal, by making a specific arrangement. In any case, be sure to consult their wishes, and if possible give yourself the pleasure of letting them make the choices. It's your choice whether you tell them about your new mindful approach.

Spend the time mindfully, giving them your full attention and relishing their company. There is no need to make notes, simply enjoy the moment.

→ Benefits of mindfulness in relationships

MORE EFFECTIVE COMMUNICATION

Being mindfully present, listening with your full attention and responding thoughtfully will all lead to more effective communication and fewer misunderstandings.

FEWER CONFLICTS

You will achieve greater empathy with others and be less likely to start or continue arguments.

LESS BROODING AND RESENTMENT

Mindfulness will help you let go of the misery that follows a difficult encounter, so that you feel less pain and are happier in yourself.

IMPROVED INSIGHT

A greater understanding of yourself and why you do the things you do will help you make changes and generally feel more comfortable in your own skin.

BETTER SOCIAL SKILLS

Mindfulness will help you stay calm and reduce any social anxiety that you may feel.

→ Dealing with difficulties

NEGATIVE THOUGHTS COMING IN DURING LOVING-KINDNESS

Inevitably when you are meditating around a difficult relationship there will be times when your thoughts drift away into brooding about the difficulties. You may start to relive anger, resentment and hurt. If this happens, gently guide your mind back to creating kindly wishes.

FEELING VULNERABLE

Where there are difficulties we often feel defensive, and as if the other person will take advantage. It can seem important not to show any weakness. The more you meditate, the stronger you will feel within yourself and the less you will worry about vulnerability. Take your time when trying to change a difficult relationship, and remember that simple mindful listening doesn't have to make you vulnerable.

BORED WHEN LISTENING

If you are naturally impatient, or so pressured that you have to do everything in a hurry, you may worry that the slower pace of mindful listening will be boring. Accept that this may happen, and remind yourself that if you give your full attention to someone you are almost bound to find something of interest.

Developing your skills

▶ Revisit the questions in Exercise 97 and record any changes in your answers. Repeat this from time to time.

▶ Repeat the loving-kindness meditation for yourself.

▶ Repeat the loving-kindness meditation for each of your relationships, regardless of how the relationship is going. Take your time over this.

▶ Extend your use of mindful listening into all aspects of your life.

▶ Continue to spend mindful time with the people you care most about.

What have I learnt?

→ What have you learnt about what you bring to relationships?

_____

_____

_____

_____

→ What have you learnt about your expectations of other people?

_____

_____

_____

_____

→ What have you learnt about mindful listening?

_____

_____

_____

_____

Where to next?

 You have reached the end of this Workbook, but the journey into mindfulness is ongoing. It's up to you how much you do, and now that you understand what mindfulness is you can start to see how it will affect your life. Some of the changes it will bring will already be obvious to you, but others will appear over time. It's an endlessly fascinating process.

Appendix 1: Body scan

1 Allow plenty of time for your first full body scan. Read through the instructions before you start. If your concentration lapses, gently bring your focus back to the exercise.

2 Spend a little time focussing on your breathing. Don't judge, just observe. Notice any changes – perhaps your breathing will quieten once you are physically relaxed, perhaps not.

3 Take stock of your body in a general way. Feel the weight of it against the chair or bed, feel the textures of clothing or covers, any draught on the skin of your face, any discomfort.

4 Focus your awareness on the big toe of your left foot. Mentally allow your next inbreath to travel down to that toe. If it helps, imagine the life-giving oxygen in your breath reaching the toe, and the waste gases leaving the toe as you breathe out. Maintain your awareness in the toe even when you breathe out, for as many breaths as you wish.

5 Keep your awareness in just that toe. Feel any sensations, whether it is warm or cold, stiff or relaxed, touching the next toe or touching clothing. Remember not to judge – you may have a bunion or callouses, you may think your toes are ugly, but right now this is just your left big toe.

6 When you are ready move on, taking your awareness to the next toe along. Repeat the process, breathing into the toe on an inbreath, keeping your awareness there when you breathe out, noticing without judging.

7 Without rushing, work your way round your entire body in the following order: all the toes of the left foot one at a time, the instep, heel and ankle. Move up into your calf and shin, your knee, and your thigh. Move across your pelvis and down into the big toe of your right foot. Repeat the sequence of individual toes, instep, heel, ankle, calf, shin, knee and thigh.

8 Take your awareness into your pelvis, then hips, buttocks and genitals. As well as being a sensitive area, this is likely to give rise to judgemental thoughts about your sexual attractiveness, habits or relationships. This is not the time for them, so let go.

9 Take your awareness to your stomach, feel it moving as you breathe. If emotions arise, allow yourself to feel them without judging, blaming, explaining or defending. Be gently interested and breathe into the emotions.

10 Move on to your chest and throat, and continue to be aware of internal and external sensations as well as any emotions.

11 When you reach your head and face take extra time for this complicated area. Start with the muscles of your face and jaw, and then take your awareness into your eyes, nose, mouth and ears. Move up to your forehead, over the top of your head and down into the back of your neck and into your shoulders.

12 Take your awareness into your left thumb followed by each finger, the palm and back of your hand, wrist, forearm, elbow and upper arm. Repeat with the right hand and arm, starting with the thumb.

13 From your right shoulder move your awareness slowly down your spine until you reach the small of your back.

14 Now imagine your awareness spreading slowly and calmly from the small of your back through your entire body. If it helps, imagine soothing warmth emanating from your back into all parts of your body. With each inward breath expand your awareness a little further into your body. Relish the sensation of harmony between your mind and your body, breathing together.

15 Now you can forget about mindfulness and the requirements of the body scan. Allow yourself to be carried by the rhythm of your breathing. Allow yourself to float.

16 When you are ready, open your eyes. Take a few moments to return to full awareness of the outside world.

 *Task sheet*

As you now understand, there are no goals in mindfulness. In one sense this is an enormous relief, since almost everything we do is goal oriented – even if the goal is just 'get this task finished'. In another sense though it can be hard to stay focussed.

While you don't need to tick every mindfulness box, it is worth reminding yourself from time to time what is available. It's easy to slip into the habit of practising only those aspects of mindfulness that appealed to you on your first reading, or only those that came easily at first. Once you have grown familiar with those practices though, and familiar with mindfulness, it's worth returning to anything that you may have skimmed or even skipped. They will have something to offer you that perhaps you weren't aware of to start with.

Use the task sheet to remind yourself of what this Workbook covers, and return to any chapters that you haven't fully absorbed, repeating the exercises.

→ Chapter 1

AUTOPILOT

Are you coming out of autopilot whenever possible, even for the most mundane of tasks?

BEING AND DOING

Do you have an understanding of the difference between Being and Doing?

Do you spend time each day just Being?

→ Chapter 2

ACKNOWLEDGEMENT

Are you beginning to fully acknowledge difficult issues?

ACCEPTANCE

Are you beginning to accept what you have acknowledged?

Do you recognize when you are in denial?

Do you let go of the second arrow of suffering?

→ Chapter 3

DETACHMENT

Are you learning to detach from your thoughts and emotions?

Have you begun to find your sense of self?

→ Chapter 4

MEDITATION: PHYSICAL

Do you maintain the quiet safe place where you meditate?

Can you improve it?

Do you have an established routine for starting and finishing your meditation sessions?

→ Chapter 5

MEDITATION: MENTAL

Are you learning to cope with quiet inactivity?

Are you learning to maintain your meditation posture?

Are you learning to let go of goals?

Can you tolerate the daily repetition of meditation?

Have you learnt to ignore distractions?

Have you learnt to stop worrying about other people?

→ Chapter 6

THREE-MINUTE BREATHING SPACE

Do you remember to use the three-minute breathing space both formally and informally?

→ Chapter 7

BODY SCAN

Do you carry out regular body scans?

Have you learnt about where in your body you feel your emotions?

→ Chapter 8

MEDITATION

Have you persevered with meditation?

Do you meet your commitment, however small?

→ Chapter 9

MINDFUL MOVEMENT

Do you practise mindful movement both formally and informally?

→ Chapter 10

LOVING-KINDNESS

Do you carry out loving-kindness meditations?

Do you extend loving-kindness to yourself?

Do you extend loving-kindness to even your most difficult relationships?

→ Chapter 11

STRESS

Do you understand your own stress?

Do you bring mindfulness to your stress?

→ Chapter 12

RELATIONSHIPS

Do you bring mindfulness to your relationships?

Do you practise mindful listening?

✚ Quick help

It can't be said too often that in mindfulness there are no exams, and no specific goals. You can't measure your achievement in any objective sense. This can feel very strange, but there are clear advantages. With no deadline (such as the date of a test) you can proceed at your own pace. It's quite common to start learning something full of energy and enthusiasm, only to tail off after a little while. Guilt sets in, you feel badly perhaps about wasted money or unfulfilled resolutions and suddenly something that started so well turns into a morass of negatives.

This need never happen with mindfulness. If you start well but tail off, allow yourself to take a break and then return to it when you're ready. There's no need for guilt or other negatives. You can follow your own natural rhythms and proceed in your own time. Even while your focus is elsewhere, during the break, your mind will continue to mull over what you've already learnt about mindfulness.

At the same time, if you feel yourself losing impetus it can be helpful to gently put yourself back on track. Here are a few suggestions and reminders.

▶ Accept that you have drifted off the mindfulness path. Allow yourself to gently return to it without guilt or recrimination.

▶ Give yourself a loving-kindness meditation. Let go of all your bad feelings.

▶ Make a conscious effort to switch off your autopilot. Choose a small task and carry it out with full mindful awareness.

▶ Stop reading this book and spend a few moments just Being. Be fully aware of the moment – your body, your feelings, your surroundings.

▶ Repeat the detachment exercises in Chapter 3.

▶ Spend some time alone in your meditation space quietly contemplating your return to meditation.

▶ Stop reading this book and take a three-minute breathing space.

▶ Stop reading this book and do a body scan.

▶ Decide when your next meditation session will be. Decide that it will be a short one and that you will meditate again the next day.

▶ Choose an activity you enjoy to practice mindful movement.

▶ Spend mindful time with someone you love.

Further resources

→ ## Taking it further

ONLINE

Mental Health Foundation

http://www.mentalhealth.org.uk/

Extensive range of publications and podcasts about mindfulness, some available for free but there is a charge for the on-line mindfulness course: http://www.bemindfulonline.com/

DISTANCE LEARNING

http://learnmindfulness.co.uk/mindfulness-courses/distance-learning-mindfulness/

FINDING RETREATS

http://www.metta.org.uk/retreats.asp

MINDFULNESS RESEARCH AND INFORMATION

http://www.mindfulexperience.org/

http://www.mindfulnet.org/

BUDDHISM

http://www.thebuddhistsociety.org/

→ ## Books

Alidina, Shamash, *Mindfulness for Dummies* (John Wiley & Sons Ltd, 2010)

Carrington, Patricia, *The Book of Meditation* (Anchor Press, 1997)

Crane, Rebecca, *Mindfulness-Based Cognitive Therapy* (Routledge, 2009)

Gunaratana, Bhante Henepola, *Mindfulness in Plain English* (Wisdom Publications, 2002)

Heaversedge, Jonty and Halliwell, Ed, *The Mindful Manifesto* (Hay House, 2010)

Kabat-Zinn, Jon, *Full Catastrophe Living (How to cope with stress, pain and illness using mindfulness meditation)* (Piatkus, 1990)

Kabat-Zinn, Jon, *Wherever You Go, There You Are (Mindfulness Meditation for Everyday Life)* (Piatkus, 1994)

Langley, Martha, *Mindfulness Made Easy* (Hodder Education, 2011)

Index

Notes